ISBN 978-1-334-23216-9
PIBN 10719291

English
Français
Deutsche
Italiano
Español
Português

www.forgottenbooks.com

Mythology Photography **Fiction**
Fishing Christianity **Art** Cooking
Essays Buddhism Freemasonry
Medicine **Biology** Music **Ancient
Egypt** Evolution Carpentry Physics
Dance Geology **Mathematics** Fitness
Shakespeare **Folklore** Yoga Marketing
Confidence Immortality Biographies
Poetry **Psychology** Witchcraft
Electronics Chemistry History **Law**
Accounting **Philosophy** Anthropology
Alchemy Drama Quantum Mechanics
Atheism Sexual Health **Ancient History**
Entrepreneurship Languages Sport
Paleontology Needlework Islam
Metaphysics Investment Archaeology
Parenting Statistics Criminology
Motivational

French.

E   he
            ne
            ls.
            ;h
            n.
            5*s*

a   at
l   nt
a   ed

b   'or
I

F
t
i   of
o   es,
7   te
           e,
           2*s*
           le.
           2*s*
           ic,
           To
           ry
           6*d*
           ;c-
           te
           :h,
           6*d*

]

]

Roget' (F. F.) Introduction to Old French. History,
  Grammar, Chrestomathy, Glossary.   Cloth   6*s*
Tarver. **Colloquial French,** for School and Private Use.
  By H. Tarver, B.-ès-L., late of Eton College. 328 pp.
  Crown 8vo. cloth   5*s*

[2]

Victor Hugo. Les Misérables. Les Principaux Episodes. Edited, with Life and Notes, by J. Boïelle, Senior French Master, Dulwich College. 2 vols. Crown 8vo. cloth   each 3s 6d

Foa (Mad. Eugen.) Contes Historiques, with idiomatic Notes by G. A. NEVEU. Second Edition. Cloth   2s

Krueger (H.) Short but Comprehensive French Grammar. 5th Edition. 180 pp. 12mo. cloth   2s

Delbos (L.) French Accidence and Minor Syntax. 2nd Edition. Crown 8vo. cloth   1s 6d

—— **Student's French Composition** on an entirely new plan. Crown 8vo. cloth   3s 6d

Strouwelle (Prof. A.) Treatise on French Genders. 12mo. cloth   1s 6d

Schmidt (Dr. H.) Petit Vocabulaire. A systematically arranged French Vocabulary of the most useful words for Exercise in Conversation. From the 25th German Edition. Cloth.   1s

Ahn's French Vocabulary and Dialogues, for English Schools. 2nd Edition. 12mo. cloth   1s 6d

Roussy. Cours de Versions. Pieces for translation into French, with Notes. Crown 8vo. cloth   2s 6d

Vinet (A.) Chrestomathie Française ou Choix de Morceaux tirés des meilleurs Ecrivains Français. 11th Edition. 358 pp. cloth   3s 6d

Williams (T. S.) and J. Lafont. French Commercial Correspondence. A Collection of Modern Mercantile Letters in French and English, with their translation on opposite pages. 2nd Edition. 12mo. cloth   4s 6d

French Classics for English Schools. Edited with Introduction and Notes by LEON DELBOS, M.A., of King's College. Crown 8vo. cloth
  1. **Racine.** Les Plaideurs   1s 6d
  2. **Corneille.** Horace   1s 6d
  3. **Corneille.** Cinna   1s 6d
  4. **Molière.** Bourgeois Gentilhomme   1s 6d
  5. **Corneille.** Le Cid   1s 6d
  6. **Molière, Les Précieuses Ridicules.**   1s 6d
  7. **Chateaubriand.** Voyage en Amérique   1s 6d
  8. **De Maistre.** Les Prisonniers du Caucase, and le Lépreux d'Aoste   1s 6d
  9. **La Fontaine's Select Fables.**   1s 6d

Fleury's Histoire de France, racontée à la Jeunesse, edited
for the use of English Pupils, with Grammatical Notes,
by Beljame. 3rd Edition. 12mo. cloth boards 3s 6d

Mandrou (A.) French Poetry for English Schools. 2nd
Edition. 12mo. cloth 2s

German.

Weisse's Complete Practical Grammar of the German
Language, with Exercises in Conversations, Letters,
&c. 4th Edition. 12mo. cloth 6s

—— **New Conversational Exercises** in German Composition, 2nd Edition. 12mo. cloth (Key, 5s) 3s 6d

Schlütter's German Class Book. A Course of Instruction
based on Becker's System, and so arranged as to
exhibit the Self-development of the Language, and its
Affinities with the English. By Fr. Schlutter, Royal
Military Academy, Woolwich. 4th Edition. 12mo.
cloth (Key 5s) 5s

Möller (A.) A German Reading Book. A Companion to
Schlutter's German Class Book. With a complete
Vocabulary. 150 pp. 12mo. cloth 2s

Ravensberg (A. v.) Practical Grammar of the German
Language. Conversational Exercises, Dialogues and
Idiomatic Expressions. Third Edition. 12mo. cloth
(Key, 2s) 5s

—— **Rose's English into German.** A Selection of Anec-
dotes, Stories, &c., with copious Notes. 2nd Edition.
Cloth (Key, 5s) 4s 6d

—— **German Reader,** Prose and Poetry, with copious
Notes for Beginners. 2nd Edition. Crown 8vo. cloth 3s

Sonnenschein and Stallybrass. First German Reading Book.
Easy Poems with interlinear Translations, Notes, etc.
4th Edition. 12mo. cloth 4s 6d

Ahn's German Method by Rose. A New Edition of the
genuine Book, with a Supplement consisting of Models
of Conjugations, a Table of all Regular Dissonant and
Irregular Verbs, Rules on the Prepositions, &c. &c.
By A. V. Rose. 2 Courses in 1 vol. Cloth 3s 6d

—— **German Method by Rose,** &c. First Course. Cloth 2s

Apel's Short and Practical German Grammar for Beginners,
with copious Examples and Exercises. 2nd Edition.
12mo. cloth 2s 6d

For Continuation see the end of the Volume.

C. JULII CÆSARIS

DE

BELLO GALLICO

LIBER I.

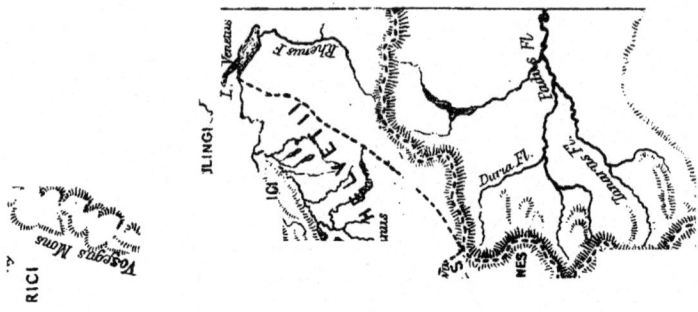
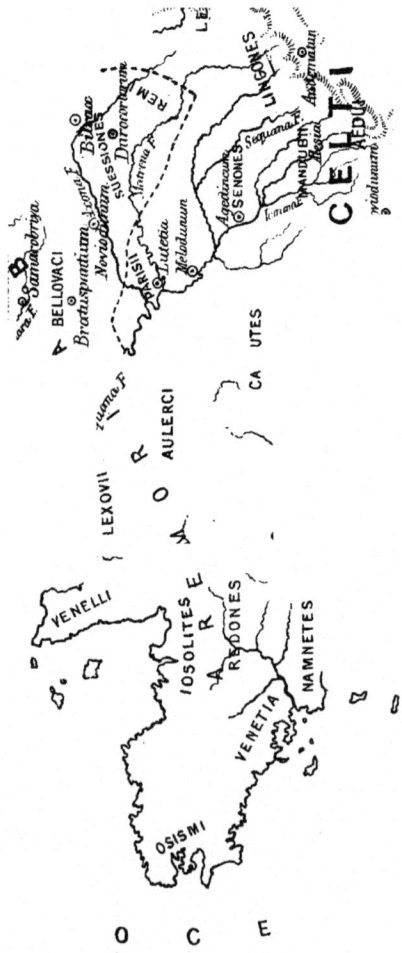
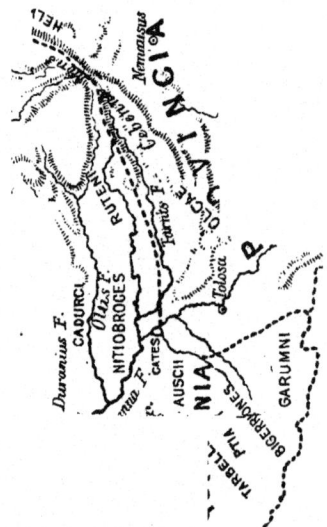

EDITED WIT:

ALEX

WIL
14. HENRIETTA

C. JULII CÆSARIS

DE

BELLO GALLICO.

LIBER PRIMUS.

EDITED WITH INTRODUCTION, NOTES, AND MAPS

BY

ALEXANDER M. BELL, M.A.,

BALL. COLL., OXON.,

WILLIAMS AND NORGATE,

14, HENRIETTA STREET, COVENT GARDEN, LONDON; AND
20, SOUTH FREDERICK STREET, EDINBURGH.

1888.

LONDON:
G. NORMAN AND SON, PRINTERS, HART STREET,
COVENT GARDEN.

CONTENTS.

PREFACE.

In this edition the text of Nipperdey has been taken as a basis; the following are the variations from this, the standard text of Cæsar; they have been adopted chiefly from the editions of Kraner and Dittenberger.

C. 3. 5. 'Æduo,' not *Hæduo*; Glück on Celtic Names. C. 5. 3. 'Rauricis,' not *Rauracis*; Glück, *ibid.* 'Latovicis,' not *Latobrigis*; Glück. C. 7. 1. 'Genavam,' not *Genuam*; Mommsen. C. 10. 4. 'Ceutrones,' not *Centrones*; Desjardins. C. 13. 5. 'contenderent' placed after *virtute*, instead of after *dolo*; Kraner. C. 17. 2, 3. 'ne frumentum conferant, quod debeant; præstare, si jam principatum Galliæ obtinere non possint, Gallorum quam Romanorum imperia perferre, neque dubitare, quin.' This conjecture, adopted from Kraner, gives a correct sentence very much in Cæsar's manner, who is partial to the impersonal use of *præstare* and to the phrase *imperia perferre*. The MS. reading, which has *præstare* before debeant, *præferre* for perferre, and a second *debeant* after dubitare, will not construe, and the word *præferre* is suspicious. C. 25. 4. 'spatio' is inserted after *passuum*. Kraner. The use of *mille* as an acc. of distance after *suberat*, and followed by a partitive genitive, is very doubtful. C. 28. 2. 'frugibus,' not *fructibus*. Frugibus has the best MS. authority, and, as the meaning is " crops of grain," it is preferable Latin. C. 31. 1. After 'secreto,' the words *in occulto*, which occur in the MS., are omitted. They are a gloss, which has crept into the text. *Secreto* means "privately," "without other witnesses than the persons concerned." That Cæsar, in the height of victory and in the heart of Gaul, could have met the Gallic chiefs " in a concealed spot," is not possible. C. 31. 9. 'Admagetobrigæ.' This, the MS. reading, is considered genuine by Mommsen; Glück's *ad Magetobrigam* is tempting on philological grounds. C. 37. 3. "Sueborum," not *Suevorum*;

Mommsen. C. 38. 3. ' mille ' is inserted before *sexcentorum*. This is Kraner's emendation, suggested by the actual measurement of the neck of land, which amounts to 1620 Roman feet. C. 39. 6. 'nuntiarant' for *nuntiabant*. MS. C. 40. 8. ' defatigatis,' not *defetigatis*. C. 47. 1. 'legatum ' for *legatis*. This reading, adopted from Rheinhard, seems called for by the words which follow, *legatum e suis*. C. 53. 1. ' quinque,' not *quinquaginta ; quinque* is the MS. reading, and the context makes it necessary. It would be hard to say why it was altered to *quinquaginta* on the authority of a passage in Orosius. *ibid.* 2. 'reppererunt' for *pepererunt*. MS. *ibid.* 4. ' Voccionis,' not *Voctionis*, Glück. ' Utraque periit,' for the MS. *utræque perierunt*. Between *duæ* and *filiæ*, ' fuerunt ' is inserted. This is a slight modification of a conjecture of Hug, adopted by Kraner, which places *fuerunt* before *duæ*. That two consecutive sentences should begin with the same words is in accordance with Cæsar's manner, and would account for the disappearance of the second *fuerunt*.

My thanks are due to Mr. Stuart Poole, the Keeper of Coins in the British Museum, and to Mr. Head, the Deputy-Keeper of Coins, for the assistance which they gave me in selecting and in having engraved the likeness of Julius Cæsar which adorns the outside and the title-page of this little book.

The likeness is taken from a large bronze of Augustus ; the inscription, Divos Julius, the divine Julius, means that Julius was dead, and had become divine. To modern ears this seems impious adulation, but to the Roman it involved no such feeling, as the worship of ancestors was a primary article of Roman faith and pious usage.

For the engraving of the coin I am indebted to Mr. F. Anderson, of 5 Newgate Street, London.

A. M. BELL.

Limpsfield, Surrey.
        August 3rd, 1887.

INTRODUCTION.

ERRATA.

c. xxxii, p. 54, *for* causa quæ, *read* "quæ causa." *ibid. after* quidem *insert* " queri."

c. xxxvi, p. 56, *for* convenissent, *read* " *convenisset.*"

c. xliv, p. 61, *for* fines, *read* "*finibus.*"

p. 68, *for* dituem, *read* " dictum."

p. 116, *for* July 16th, *read* " July 16th—Aug. 11th."

hundred years. About the year 600 B.C., Bellovese, a prince of the Bituriges, at that time the most powerful Celtic tribe, had summoned to his standard the superabundant population of the most warlike and adventurous communities of Gaul. The vast horde, swelled by troops of women and children—for this was no ordinary invading army, but a wandering population in search of a new home,— the knightly class, a large proportion of the host, mounted on horses in which they took excessive pleasure and pride, entered Italy by the pass of the Lesser St. Bernard and the long and steep valley of the Dora Baltea. This mountain torrent, impetuously descending from its impenetrable home

Mommsen. C. 38. 3. ' mille ' is inserted before *sexcentorum*.
This is Kraner's emendation, suggested by the actual measurement of the neck of land, which amounts to 1620 Roman
feet. C. 39. 6. ' nuntiarant ' for *nuntiabant*. MS. C. 40. 8.
' defatigatis,' not *defetigatis*. C. 47. 1. 'legatum ' for *legatis*.
This reading, adopted from Rheinhard, seems called for by
the words which follow, *legatum e suis*. C. 53. 1. ' quinque,'
not *quinquaginta ; quinque* is the MS. reading, and the context makes it necessary. It would be hard to say why it

in selecting and in having engraved the likeness of Julius
Cæsar which adorns the outside and the title-page of this
little book.

The likeness is taken from a large bronze of Augustus ;
the inscription, Divos Julius, the divine Julius, means that
Julius was dead, and had become divine. To modern ears
this seems impious adulation, but to the Roman it involved
no such feeling, as the worship of ancestors was a primary
article of Roman faith and pious usage.

For the engraving of the coin I am indebted to Mr. F.
Anderson, of 5 Newgate Street, London.

                                        A. M. BELL.
Limpsfield, Surrey.
        August 3rd, 1887.

INTRODUCTION.

———————✦———————

Rome and Gaul.

The Gauls in Italy.—In the early times of the monarchy
and aristocratic rule, when the Roman State was developing
the political and military institutions destined either to crush
or to absorb every nation of the western world, hosts of
invaders had already descended into Italy from the north,
whose advancing steps seemed at first to be irresistible.
They were the Celts, the inhabitants of central and northern
Gaul. Roman tradition tells how the rich plains of
Lombardy were won by these invaders from their previous
possessors, the Etruscans, and completely occupied by means
of a series of invasions, which lasted over a period of two
hundred years. About the year 600 B.C., Bellovese, a
prince of the Bituriges, at that time the most powerful
Celtic tribe, had summoned to his standard the superabundant population of the most warlike and adventurous
communities of Gaul. The vast horde, swelled by troops of
women and children—for this was no ordinary invading
army, but a wandering population in search of a new home,—
the knightly class, a large proportion of the host, mounted
on horses in which they took excessive pleasure and pride,
entered Italy by the pass of the Lesser St. Bernard and the
long and steep valley of the Dora Baltea. This mountain
torrent, impetuously descending from its impenetrable home

among the snows of Mont Blanc, breaking and bursting the solid rocks in its onward course, and spreading devastation upon the plains beneath, offers no inadequate emblem of the power of the invading horde. The Tuscans were conquered in a great and decisive battle, and driven from their possessions, when the town of *Mediolanium*, the modern Milan, was founded by the conquerors. A second horde soon followed, when the *Cenomani* made themselves masters of the district between Brescia and Verona. By these two invasions all Italy north of the Po was secured to the Gauls. After the lapse, probably, of several generations, the Boians and Lingons followed, crossed the Po, and conquered the land between the Apennines and the Po.

Ere long Gaul was to be in contact with Rome. In the year 391 B.C., the *Senones*, who had formed settlements upon the Umbrian shore of the Adriatic, crossed the Apennines, and while engaged before the walls of Clusium against their old enemies the Etruscans, recognized mingling in the fray the too-warlike ambassadors of Rome. This gave them a new enemy, and in the ensuing year, B.C. 390, they descended to the heart of Italy, met and confounded the Roman legions at the Allia, and, on the succeeding days, sacked and burned the eternal city.

Such was the first encounter of the Gaul and the Roman. For centuries to come the Gallic broadsword and lance, the close-fitting breeches and flowing plaids of striped tartan, the blue eyes, russet hair, and tall frames, above all the fierce and almost irresistible onset of the fearless Gaul, was the true terror of the Roman statesman, citizen, or legionary.

The Romans were able to learn the lessons of adversity. " *Strange is the fortune allotted to us by destiny* "—Livy places these words in the mouth of Scipio Africanus,—" *in every great war we have been defeated and yet victorious.* " This truth, so glorious to the Roman national character, is admirably illustrated by the relations between Rome and

Gaul. After the fatal day of the Allia, the Gauls gained
many victories over Rome, but were more often defeated ;
their own victories were fruitless, but the victories of Rome
were followed up by the planting of colonies and the construction of military roads, till they ended in the complete
triumph of subjugation and peace, and the conquered were
absorbed amongst the conquerors.

Between the years 361 and 349 B.C., Livy mentions
repeated conflicts with the Gauls, in all of which, according
to his account, the first charge of the Gauls produced
hesitation and fear in the Roman ranks, but the skill of the
Roman general at last secured victory. In the first of these
conflicts the youthful Titus Manlius acquired the surname
of Torquatus from the *torque*, or large ring of gold which he
took off the Gallic chief whom he had slain in single combat,
in presence of the Gallic and Roman hosts. This champion of Gaul had held his Italian antagonists so cheap,
that in challenging them to battle he stepped before the
Roman lines, putting out his tongue in childish defiance. In
349 B.C., L. Valerius Corvus gained a similar trophy. The
Roman *gladius* was proving a match for the Celtic broadsword.

Fifty years of peace followed, till in the year 295 B.C. the
Roman legions met the united powers of Italy on the field
of Sentinum. Samnites, Etruscans, Umbrians, and Gauls
were all banded together against the Roman name. On that
day Roman virtue prevailed ; the devotion of Decius, and
the wise tactics of his colleague Fabius, gained a decisive
victory, which left Rome virtually mistress of the Italian
peninsula. It still remained to follow up the advantage, to
pursue the isolated tribes, and conquer them in their own
districts and strongholds. The first step was taken in
B.C. 283, when the Senones were annihilated, and the defeat
of the Allia expiated. Wars with Pyrrhus and Carthage
intervened, and two generations passed before the Romans

were able to reduce the north of Italy under their rule. It was not till B.C. 222 that M. Claudius Marcellus gained the *spolia opima* by slaying with his own hand Viridomar, the Insubrian chief, and, by his victory at Clastidium, conquered the valley of the Po. Two colonies were at once planted, Placentia and Cremona, which secured the power of Rome over Cisalpine Gaul.

The Italian Gauls, no longer independent, gave some assistance to Hannibal in the Second Punic War. At the Thrasymene it was an Insubrian knight, Ducar, who slew the gallant consul Flaminius, and at Cannæ the hardest of the fighting fell upon Hannibal's Gallic troops.

The Romans in Gaul.—With the ensuing century the invading tide sets northwards, and the Romans are the aggressors. Italy, Sicily, Africa, and Spain were under their rule, so that, to maintain undisputed supremacy in the western Mediterranean, it was necessary to secure at least the sea-board of Gaul. Fear also of their Gallic enemy, and of the passage of the Alps, had in great measure passed away. When therefore, in 154 B.C., the people of Marseilles requested the assistance of Rome against the neighbouring Gallic tribes, the request was readily granted, and the enemies of Marseilles were silenced. But the Romans were satisfied with securing the friendship of the ancient city, the depôt of the commerce of the Rhone valley, and allowed a generation to pass before they made any permanent settlement upon Gallic soil. In B.C. 123, the Allobroges, a brave and powerful tribe, whose lands extended from Geneva to the Isère, were defeated by Sextius Calvinus near Aix, where Aquæ Sextiæ was founded, the first Roman fortress in Further Gaul. In the next year the Arvernians (*Auvergne*), at that time the leading tribe of Southern Gaul, appeared in the field with the Allobroges, but the united host was defeated by the consul Cn. Domitius Ahenobarbus, in a great battle near Avignon; after which, Betuitus, the

Arvernian king, was decoyed to Italy, and kept a prisoner there by the treacherous action of the senate. In B.C. 121, a decisive battle, fought by Q. Fabius Maximus at the junction of the Isère and the Rhone, completed the destruction of the Allobrogians, whose lands were occupied by the conquerors, and became the first portion of the Roman Province of Further Gaul. It was in these conflicts that the Æduans (*Autun*), a powerful tribe of central Gaul, the hereditary rivals of the Arvernians, entered into alliance and friendship with the Romans, and, with true Celtic vanity, invented fables which connected their origin with the legendary stories of the foundation of Rome. In B.C. 118 the consul Q. Marcius Rex conquered the Volcæ (*Languedoc*), and the borders of the Province were extended to Tolosa (*Toulouse*). In the same year was founded the colony of Narbo Martius (*Narbonne*), which was the capital of the Province and the seat of government. The bounds of the Province were not altered until after Cæsar's conquests; its principal features, the fortress of Aix and the capital, Narbonne, with two arms of land extending on one side to Geneva and on the other to Toulouse, show clearly that the primary object in the establishment of the Province was to possess the Mediterranean sea-board and the two natural highroads which lead to the coast from the interior, and in this way to secure the route to Spain.

Although no additions were made to the Roman dominions in Gaul during the ensuing sixty years, the power of the native tribes did not increase; their lands were attacked by an enemy more terrible than Rome had hitherto proved. The Cimbrian horde for a number of years before their invasion of Italy had overrun and devastated Gaul; only the warlike Belgians of the north had resisted them with success. The Romans attempted to stem the invading tide before it reached the borders of Italy, but in vain; in B.C. 113, the consul Carbo was defeated at Noreia; in 109, Silanus met

the same fate in southern Gaul; in 107, the consul, L. Cassius Longinus, met a division of the Helvetians, now in alliance with the Cimbrians, in the lands of the Nitiobroges; he and his legate, the ex-consul Gaius Piso, fell on the battlefield with the best part of his army, and the remnant was only saved by passing beneath the yoke and by giving hostages.

A more crushing defeat upon Gallic soil was in store for Rome. In B.C. 105, two consular armies, under Q. Servilius Cæpio and Cn. Mallius Maximus, faced the Cimbrians at Arausio (*Orange*); in the conflict which followed eighty thousand Roman soldiers and forty thousand camp-followers are said to have perished, and, for the moment, the Province was lost to Rome. Since the day of Cannæ no such disaster had befallen the Roman arms.

Marius repaired these losses by destroying the Teutons at Aquæ Sextiæ (102), and the Cimbrians on the Raudine plain (101); and Rome was relieved from the fear of a second *dies Alliensis*. The Cimbrian invasion may at first sight appear to have passed away without leaving any lasting effect, like some vast volcanic disturbance, which for a moment supersedes and overthrows the ordinary operations of nature, spreading destruction for a time, but disappearing to leave no very material alteration on the surface of the soil. In reality the Cimbrian invasion had important consequences; the Gallic tribes were shattered and broken, and were taught to be defeated within their own borders; the successes of the invaders in Gaul were an invitation to other Germanic tribes, still half-nomad in their habits, to cross the Rhine · while to the Roman statesman the facts were at once a warning of the imminent danger to Rome which lurked in the impenetrable forests beyond the Rhine, and an indication of a great policy of conquest and colonization. The principles of such a policy had already been the inspiration of Caius Gracchus, and had led to the occupation of the

Roman Province of Further Gaul. Marius had neither the time nor the capacity to take up the interrupted work of his great predecessor; he was satisfied with restoring the Province to Rome, and with repelling for one or two generations the danger of a northern invasion of Italy. After the last victory of Marius no further step was taken in Gaul for forty-three years, owing to the Italian wars.

In the year 63 B.C., the Allobroges besought the senate for relief from the oppression of governors and usurers; they were asked by Catiline to join in his conspiracy, but refused to do so. Their fidelity was not rewarded, for their requests were not granted, and in 61 they rose in rebellion and seized Vienna.* The prætor, Pomptinus, with difficulty induced them to lay down arms.

In the ensuing year, in B.C. 60, there was again disquieting news from Gaul. The Helvetians, it was rumoured, were arming, and making great and careful preparations for an invasion of Gaul in search of new settlements. The danger to the Province was imminent, as it was the Tigurini, a single division of the Helvetian tribe, who in B.C. 107 had defeated Cassius, a defeat which had heralded the temporary loss of the Province. Divico, who had commanded the victorious army so many years before, was now in his old age one of the leaders of the proposed emigration.

Even more dangerous was the actual state of affairs in Northern Gaul, for the German tribes had not been slow to read the lesson taught by the Cimbrian invasion. Already in the year 72 Ariovistus had crossed the Rhine, at the head of a powerful host. Cæsar calls him a Suebian, and his followers Suebians, but it is probable that they came from a number of tribes, and that the name Suebian is an

---

* The modern *Vienne*, situated on the Rhone nineteen miles below Lyons. It must not be confused with the capital of Austria, the Latin name of which is *Vindobona*.

appellative title, meaning the Wanderers or Adventurers (*schwelen*, to hover ; *schweifen*, to rove). Ariovistus had been invited by the Arvernians and Sequans to aid them in their rivalry with the Æduans. Ere long more Germans crossed over, when it was found that the invited friend was the more dangerous foe. In a great battle fought in B.C. 61, at an uncertain spot, Admagetobriga, the great hill or *brae*, but probably in the upper basin of the Saône, Ariovistus signally defeated the Æduans and the Celtic confederation of which they were the head, and in the hour of victory showed to the Sequans that they had only secured his assistance at the price of their own independence. Two-thirds of Sequan land was demanded for German occupants. The Æduans implored the senate to assist them, the old allies and brothers of Rome. Divitiacus, a venerable Druid of high rank, went to Rome to plead the cause of his country. He had an interview with Cicero, and conversed with him on religious ceremonial and belief ; but in spite of this personally friendly reception, his request was refused, and on a motion of Cæsar, the presiding consul, the senate conferred on Ariovistus the title of king and friend of the Roman people.

Such was the position of Gaul; hereditary rivalries debarred national union; a German invader had defeated the flower of the Celtic nobility, and occupied Celtic soil with an army of 100,000 men; a vast emigration, foreboding unknown dangers, threatened the land, when in the year 58 B.C., Julius Cæsar, after the completion of his consulate, appeared in the Gallic Province as proconsul.

Julius Cæsar.

Caius Julius Cæsar, the newly appointed proconsul, did not at first sight appear to be a governor more than usually dangerous to the liberties of Gaul. He was forty-two years of age, and although he had already distinguished himself in the field both as a soldier and as a commander, the greater portion of his energy had been given to political struggles, so that, while a superficial observer might have thought that his heart was with the polished, voluptuous life of the city, and his ambition bounded by the admiration of the venal populace of Rome, not even the most sagacious could have divined that he was about to display, for nine years in succession, every power of the highest military genius.

He was born, in the year 100 B.C., of an old patrician stock. The Julian house was one of those *gentes,* which were said to have been incorporated with the more purely Roman families after the conquest of Alba Longa, and from the earliest days of the republic members of the Julian family had borne high office. Cæsar himself was not insensible to the distinction of his birth, as the following words prove; they were spoken at the funeral of his father's sister, and were long afterwards remembered in Rome. *" By the mother's side my aunt Julia sprang from kings, by the father's side she was connected with the gods. For the line of the Marcii Reges, to whom her mother belonged, is descended from Ancus Martius; while the Julian line, to which my own family belongs, is from Venus. Our house therefore possesses both the dignity of kings, whose power is greatest among men, and the sanctity of gods, to whom even kings must bow."* The aunt at whose funeral these words were spoken was the wife of Caius Marius. This connection had more influence on Cæsar's career than either his patrician birth or the political traditions of the Julian house. Among the earliest recollections of his childhood must have been his uncle's halls, adorned with the uncouth spoils of the Cimbrian and Teuton tribes, and even more adorned by the stern figure of the aged warrior; and his boyish imagination must have been charmed and terrified by stories which told of the courage and skill which had freed Rome from a fearful danger, still fresh in the memories of the narrators. Marius, before his death in B.C. 86, appointed his nephew, though only fourteen years old, Flamen Dialis, and with the priestly mantle so laid upon his shoulders the boy at once assumed much of the spirit of his uncle. He showed very soon how firmly he had chosen his position as a follower of Marius and a hereditary opponent of the aristocracy. In B.C. 82, when he was only seventeen, he repudiated Cossutia, the wife to whom his father had betrothed him, and married Cornelia, daughter of L. Cinna, the chief opponent of the dictator Sulla. Sulla saw the power latent in his stripling antagonist, and ordered him to put away Cornelia. When obedience was refused, he deprived the youthful Cæsar of his priesthood, of his wife's dower, of his own private fortune, and proscribed his name. Cæsar fled from Rome, and, lurking in the Sabine country, had to buy his life from an assassin. The Vestal Virgins and other friends at last obtained a pardon for him from the dictator. But to the plea of his boyish insignificance Sulla replied in the well-known answer: *"You have no eyes, if you do not see many Mariuses in this boy."*

Cæsar, on receiving his pardon, at once left Rome, and took service in the army under the proprætor M. Minucius Thermus, who in 81 B.C. was conducting the siege of Mitylene, which still held out for Antiochus. The city fell in the ensuing year, and Cæsar showed such conspicuous courage in the storm, that his general awarded him a civic crown, for saving the life of a Roman citizen. This was his first acquaintance with war.

Sulla died in 78 B.C., and at the news Cæsar returned to the capital, where he spent the next twenty years of his life

almost continuously, devoting himself entirely to political
affairs. Immediately on his return he gave evidence that he
possessed a discernment and self-restraint rare in a youth of
twenty-two, by refusing to identify himself with the fortunes
of any recognized leader or party. At the same time he
assumed an independent position as a partisan of the popular
cause by the impeachment of Dolabella, an adherent of Sulla,
for extortion in the government of Macedonia. The jury
of senators, in whose eyes the extortion of a distant province
was a very venial offence, refused to convict Dolabella; still
the laurels of the trial rested with the youthful orator,
whose eloquence and power pointed him out to the demo
cracy as a future leader.

Aware of his own genius, Cæsar desired to possess
political power, which could only at that time be obtained by
popularity with the electors of Rome, a venal and pleasure-
loving crowd. Lavish distributions of money soon brought
his private fortune to an end, yet he still continued to
spend immense sums for the amusement of the populace.
So great was his credit, or, in other words, the usurers
foresaw so strong a guarantee of repayment in the promise
of his career, that he is said to have been 1300 talents, or
£300,000, in debt, before he attained to any public office.
Yet Plutarch's comment is just: " *To all appearance he was
courting ruin to obtain a short-lived popularity; in reality he
was securing the greatest possessions for trifles.*"

The grateful public showered honour after honour upon
him; he was successively elected military tribune, quæstor,
curule ædile, Pontifex Maximus, prætor, and consul. The
office of Chief Pontiff, which was one of the highest social
dignities of Rome, and conferred besides the substantial
power of a regulating influence over the public sacrifices,
was usually reserved for the closing honour of some venerable aristocratic leader. That it should be wrested from the
senatorial party, and bestowed on a youthful democrat of 37,

who had as yet had no career beyond the walls of Rome, appeared at first incredible.   Q. Lutatius Catulus was the candidate of the aristocracy, who, on finding out the great popularity of his rival and fearing his own defeat, offered to pay Cæsar's debts, if he would withdraw from the contest. *" I will borrow more, and beat you,"* was Cæsar's reply.   Yet the burden of his debts was pressing heavily on Cæsar ; on the morning of the election, as he kissed his mother Aurelia and left his house, his parting words were, *" Mother, you will see me Chief Pontiff to-day, or an exile."*   The result revealed his popularity ; for he polled more votes from his opponent's tribes than they did from all the tribes together.

His chief acts in his various offices were the honour which he conferred on the memory of Marius, the repeal of Sulla's enactments, the re-establishment of the tribunate of the commons, and the alienation of Pompey from the senatorial party, his natural friends.   Although Cæsar could not foresee the future or his own destiny, throughout all his career there reigns a definite purpose, which was not altered either by the overtures of friends, the mistakes of enemies, or by his own successes.   We shall not probably err in supposing that he had the lives of Caius Gracchus and of Marius before him, and while he regarded both as his patterns and predecessors, he was determined to attain the strength, and to avoid the weakness of both.   Like Gracchus, he intended to enlarge the borders and the sympathies of Roman. civilization ; but he would not, as Gracchus had done, lean solely on the support of a venal and fickle populace.   Like Marius, he was resolved to triumph over the aristocracy, and also to save the state from foreign dangers, but it was alien to his nature to degrade a great genius, as Marius had done, to the level of his meanest opponents, and, by staining himself with cruelty, to sow the seed of undying dissensions ; Cæsar had *" a generous and a gentle spirit"* (*clemens et mitis natura*).   He saw that the principles which had animated the republic existed no longer, and amid the anarchy of factions, and of selfish and bloody combinations, of which the conspiracy of Catiline (B.C. 63) is a type, and not an isolated and accidental phenomenon, he was conscious that he was born to rule, and appointed to inaugurate a new era of Roman life; very probably at an early period in his career the idea floated before his mind, gradually to become fixed in more definite and permanent shape, that to obtain power by popular favour and to secure it by the support of devoted legionaries was the only means by which to make an attempt for the regeneration of the Roman world.

Cæsar's quæstorship (B.C. 68), and his proprætorship (B.C. 61) were both spent in Spain. At the time when he obtained the latter appointment he was forty years of age, and had never commanded an army; yet he at once proved his military ability by subduing the wild mountaineers of Gallicia and Portugal (*Gallæci* and *Lusitani*), and he caused the arm of Roman authority to be felt as far as the Atlantic. Victorious in the field, Cæsar was saluted as *imperator* by his triumphant troops, and he acquired similar fame by the civil administration of his province. He is said also to have enriched his army, and to have returned to Rome able to pay his debts. By what means so vast a sum of money could be procured in a single year of office, it 'is better only guessing.' Suetonius says expressly: "*He was not spotless in his administration either of military or of civil power. Certain writers assert in their memoirs that as proconsul in Spain he accepted from friendly states sums of money which he had asked for to relieve his own debts, and that he allowed his soldiers to sack certain towns of the Lusitanians, which were so far from refusing obedience, that they opened their gates to him.*" We may hope that the latter assertion is an exaggeration of an opponent, for political pens were not scrupulous in Rome. The first accusation is perhaps true, but finds some palliation in the use which Cæsar made of the extorted gold. He had no vulgar love of money, which was in his eyes but the necessary means to further vast and beneficent designs.

In the year 59 Cæsar was consul, when the contentions between him and the senate so far surpassed the proportions of ordinary party strife that it was plain that arms at last would end the quarrel. Yet Cæsar always knew how to be victorious. Bibulus, his senatorial colleague, was reduced during half his consulate to such a nonentity that the city wags, in writing to each other, dated their letters *" in the consulate of Julius and Cæsar,"* and other witticisms flew about. The senate had passed a resolution that the " woods and pastures " should be the province of the outgoing consul, a duty in which, of course, no distinction could be gained. Cæsar could neither brook the insult nor meet it single-handed. He therefore entered into a private arrangement with Pompey and Crassus, which has been called the First Triumvirate. The terms of the agreement were,—*" That nothing of a public nature should be done, which was unsatisfactory to any one of the three."* The chief bills passed by Cæsar in his consulate were an agrarian law, which divided lands in Italy among twenty thousand of the poorer citizens, many of them Pompey's veterans, and a law which granted the publicans relief from some too onerous contracts which they had undertaken. These bills procured for Cæsar popularity both with the richer and the poorer classes in Rome, so that when Vatinius, the tribune, brought a bill before the people asking that the provinces of Cisalpine Gaul and Illyricum with command of three legions should be conferred on Cæsar for five years, it was readily passed. The senate added to this the government of Transalpine Gaul for the same period, with command of an additional legion. They did so from no love to Cæsar, but because they were aware that, if they did not make the addition, the people would, and they yielded when they could yield with a good grace. Doubtless they hoped that the casualties of war might relieve them of their hitherto invincible antagonist; indeed emissaries from various nobles were ere long on the way to Ariovistus, the German king, and the object of their mission was to set a price on Cæsar's head.

After the close of his consulate Cæsar stayed near Rome for some months, waiting till Cicero left the city in exile. Towards the close of April Cæsar's departure was precipitated by the news that the Helvetian tribe was about to march through the Roman Province on their way to find fresh settlements in Gaul. He left Rome hastily, and in eight days reached Geneva.

There can be no doubt that Cæsar entered Gaul with the definite purpose of not leaving the country until he had subjected every tribe to the rule of Rome, and thereby put a close to a long rivalry, and set the Italian Peninsula free, apparently for ever, from the danger of being overrun by some fresh northern horde. This end was final in itself; it was a national desire, and shared by Romans of every party. In another light Cæsar as plainly meditated the conquest of Gaul as a means to attain further ends, and merely as a step in his own career as a Roman statesman. The events of the preceding year had made it clear to less discerning observers than Cæsar that the anarchy of the senatorial government could not continue, nor yet be brought to an end, except by a strong hand. Cæsar now knew from experience of years what he had originally felt in the consciousness of genius, that he was born to govern and to control, and his late campaign in Further Spain had inspired him with confidence in his military powers, and with the desire of obtaining more military glory, and, as a consequence, unbounded popularity with a devoted army. The spoils of Gaul were also in his eye, for the temples of the rich land were still unsacked; and the treasures of gold deposited there were, he well knew, one of the only existing sources from which he could pour a stream of new and bewildering munificence on the astonished multitudes of Rome. This is not a conjecture of malevolence; Suetonius writes :—" *In Gaul he plundered temples and shrines laden with gifts, and frequently plundered cities, without any offence of the inhabitants, for the sake of the booty. The result was that he possessed himself of gold in abundance, and sold it throughout Italy and the provinces for three thousand sesterces the pound.*"*

To our eyes the entrance of a nominally friendly country with the resolution to destroy its ancient liberties has the appearance of treachery and high-handed aggression; to the Roman of the time the facts bore a very different aspect than they bear when viewed in the light of modern politics. It was an axiom among Roman statesmen that Rome was destined to rule and other nations to obey ; *tu regere imperio populos, Romane, memento.* The Gauls, among all the hereditary enemies of Rome, were now the most ancient, and had been the most dangerous. Disturbed as their land was by internal dissensions, that did not imply to the Roman that his country should stand aloof, but rather enter the arena and by pacifying the combatants underneath her own rule, prevent the land from becoming the prey of the more dangerous barbarians who were already appearing on the Rhine frontier. The popular sentiment in Rome is clearly and eloquently expressed by Cicero in a speech, *De Provinciis Consularibus,* which he delivered in the senate four years after Cæsar's entry into Gaul, in favour of the proposal that Cæsar's pro-consular power should be prolonged for five additional years. Cæsar had by this time committed the doubtful acts of his career ; he had sold the Venetans into slavery, and had treacherously—for we cannot otherwise regard his act—annihilated the Usipetes and Tencteri, men, women, and children together. Cicero does not speak of these acts ; he only sees in Cæsar the conqueror of an ancient enemy, and

---

* The ordinary value was four thousand sesterces, or nearly so ; *libra* = 40 *aurei, aureus* = 25 *denarii, denarius* = 4 *sestertii.*

the dissipater of an ancient fear. *" In former days, my lords,"* thus he addresses the senate, *"we held but a military road through Gaul; the rest of the country was in the hands of tribes either hostile to our rule, or faithless, or unknown; they were at all events wild, savage, and warlike. No one has ever failed to desire the conquest and subjection of these rude tribes. From the early days of our history no wise Roman statesman has not considered that Gaul was the chief danger to our empire, only, owing to the power and numbers of the Gallic tribes, we have never before now faced their united strength."*

Cæsar was a Roman, and shared these views; indeed, he saw more clearly than other Romans that the danger from the Germans on the Rhine frontier already threatened Italy very nearly; and he entered his Province with the resolution of conquering Gaul, not merely to secure the ends of his personal ambition, but to give full and lasting effect to the traditional policy of Rome.

Suetonius describes the person of the proconsul in the following words ·—*" He was tall in figure, of a fair complexion, and with shapely limbs; his mouth was somewhat thick-lipped, his eyes dark and animated, and his general health excellent. He was unusually particular of his personal appearance, carefully using not only the razor and the pumice, but even tweezers. with which he was sometimes taunted; he was bald, and very sensitive of the defect, which frequently made him the butt of disparaging jests."*

" He was a perfect master of his arms and of his horse, and capable of enduring incredible fatigue. On the march he was at the head of his army, sometimes on horseback, but more usually on foot, with his head bare, in spite of either sun or rain."

" In addressing his troops he did not call them soldiers, but by the gentler title, ' My fellow-soldiers,*' and he loved them so much that, on hearing of the loss of the division under Titurius, he allowed his hair and beard to grow, remaining untrimmed*

until their death was expiated. By these means he made their courage and their devotion to himself very great."

Of his manners the ancients say little; it is perhaps enough to know that he possessed the charm which is inseparable from genius; that his natural sympathies were many-sided, and were enlarged by his versatile energy and constant intercourse with the world ; and that his daily conversation was not only witty, sparkling, and brilliant, but possessed the grace of gentleness combined with strength. Standing alone in the isolation of his genius, he showed distinction in his look and bearing, and even *hauteur* ; yet he was not repellent, for all his associates felt that he could be trusted; *" I am Cæsar, and will keep my word,"* was his saying to an adversary, and it was never falsified.

State of Gaul, 58 B.C.

The country known to the Romans as Gallia, or Gaul, embraced the dominions of France, Switzerland, Belgium, and part of Holland, together with the German provinces west of the Rhine. Its boundaries were the Ocean and the Mediterranean, the Pyrenees, the Alps, and the Rhine, the same limits as modern France possessed between the years 1793 and 1813. This great territory was under no central government ; the Romans had already reduced a portion, which formed the Province of Further Gaul (*Provence*) ; in independent Gaul there were three great divisions, Aquitania, Gallia Belgica, and Gallia Celtica ; while German tribes had appropriated a considerable strip of Gallic soil on the left bank of the Rhine.

The Roman Province extended along the Mediterranean coast from the Alps to the Pyrenees. It was, as Cicero describes it, a military road through Gaul (*semita Galliæ*), connecting Italy with Spain. The chief posts on this highway were Aquæ Sextiæ (*Aix*) on the Italian, and Narbo Martius (*Narbonne*) on the Pyrenean frontier; between them lay Massilia (*Marseilles*), a friendly town, the chief emporium of the commerce of Gaul. Aquæ Sextiæ, as has already been said, was the first Roman establishment in Gaul; it was not a residential town but a fortress (*castellum*), raised in 123 B.C. to secure fruitful and permanent results from the victory of Sextius Calvinus over the Allobrogians. Massilia, the ancient colony of the hardy sailors of Phocæa, had given Rome very important assistance in her wars with Hannibal, and had experienced similar aid against her own Gallic neighbours in return. The city was not subject to Rome, but was under a treaty (*fœderata civitas*), and was always a friend and hearty ally; Cicero describes it twice in the same words as "*the city without whose aid our commanders never gained a victory over the Transalpine tribes.*" Indeed, as a basis of communication with Italy, and as a centre for obtaining supplies, Marseilles may almost be named the heart of the Province. Narbo was the name of an ancient Celtic town, but when in B.C. 118 it received a colony of Roman citizens, it received the name of Narbo Martius, the town of Mars. It was an outpost town, whose inhabitants, although traders with the Gauls and cultivators of the soil, made their bargains and trimmed their vines with the sword by their side. Cicero names it as "*a colony of Roman citizens, a watch-tower and bulwark of Rome, resisting and confronting the wild tribes of those regions.*"* Narbo was the capital of the Roman Province, a proof that the Province was not established with a view to the conquest of Gaul so much as to hold the route to Spain. The fact that Cæsar did not visit Narbo till the seventh year of the war, when its existence was endangered, is a proof that he entered the Province with different intentions than previous governors.

The Province extended up the Rhone valley as far as the

---

* *Pro Fonteio. c. 1. Colonia nostrorum civium, specula Populi Romani et propugnaculum, istis ipsis nationibus oppositum et objectum.*

town of Genava (*Geneva*). The line of the Rhone was the frontier, assumed for military reasons after the conquest of the Allobrogians, and successfully maintained by Cæsar in his first campaign, and again by Lucius Cæsar in the seventh year of the war. There were many important towns in the Rhone valley; Arelate (*Arles*), an ancient town of the Salyes; Arausio (*Orange*), of the Cavari; and Nemausus (*Nismes*), the old capital of the Volcæ Arecomici. Vienna (*Vienne*) was the chief town of the Allobrogians; in Roman hands it was an important military post, near enough the frontier for observation, and sufficiently distant to be safe from surprise. In all these towns the Roman influence now prevailed; the most important men among the native population had been proud to receive the citizenship of Rome, and gave Cæsar most hearty support throughout his campaigns.

To the west the Province included Tolosa (*Toulouse*), on the upper course of the Garonne. This position at first sight appears isolated and insecure, but is in reality necessary to ensure the safety of the Mediterranean coast. Two routes from central Gaul lead to the Mediterranean; one is by the Rhone valley, which the Romans had secured : the other is created by a depression of the land between the sinking spurs of the Pyrenees and the rising ridges of the Cevennes, and extends from Toulouse by Carcassonne to Narbonne. The depression is so important a natural feature of the country that for the past two hundred years it has been traversed by the *Canal du Midi*, which, beginning at Toulouse and ending at Agde, connects the Mediterranean with the Atlantic. This natural highway could not be left open to the warlike Aquitanians or to the Celtic Gauls, and in occupying Toulouse, and choosing the line of the upper Garonne as their frontier, the Romans only did what was necessary to secure their hold upon the coast. The repulse of the invasion threatened in B.C. 52 proved that the line of defence was well selected, and could be successfully maintained by the militia of the Province.

Aquitania.—The three divisions of independent Gaul all differed from each other in language, in social customs, and in laws. Aquitania was the smallest and the least important of these divisions ; Cæsar did not enter it in person until the eighth year of the war. Aquitania was the district between the Pyrenees and the Garonne, westward of Toulouse. Even in this region the Aquitanians had been forced to retire from a strip of land at the mouth of the Garonne, where the Bituriges Vivisci, a tribe of Celtic Gaul, had effected a settlement, and founded the town Burdigăla (*Bordeaux*).

The chief Aquitanian tribes are the Garumni (*Garonne*), the Bigerriones (*Bigorre*), the Auscii (*Auch*), the Ptianii, Tarbelli, Sontiates (*Sos*), Tarusates, Sibuzates (*Saulusse*), Cocosates. These names have a distinctive sound, different from the appellatives of Celtic Gauls, and there is no doubt that the Aquitanians were not Celts, but the remnants of an earlier race. Their affinities were with Spain, rather than with Gaul, for when Crassus attacked Aquitania, the inhabitants received important assistance from the Cantabrian tribes, whereas the Aquitanians held entirely aloof from Gaul in the great rising under Vercingetorix. They were, no doubt, the ancestors of the Basques of modern times, who live in the Pyrenean valleys both of France and Spain, still retaining their ancient language, and marked by peculiar mental as well as physical characteristics. They are short in stature, swarthy in complexion, and in their habits cunning and deceitful ; little disposed to agriculture and to commerce, but ever distinguished, from the days of Hannibal to the days of Napoleon, as hardy foot-soldiers, faithfully retaining, on the sultry plains of Italy or of Austria, the active habits and the lithe forms bred in their native mountain-valleys. Their language does not belong to the Indo-European class,

which embraces the Latin and Greek, Celtic and German,
but it is of an earlier type. These three facts, the distinctive physical features of the race, their peculiar and
isolated language, and the geographical position of their
home, all point to the conclusion that the Basques of to-day
or the Aquitanians of Cæsar's time are a remnant of an
earlier population, who, unable to face the hordes of invading
Celts, found in the desolate heaths and forests which extend
from Bordeaux to Bayonne, and in the inaccessible valleys
of the Pyrenees, a shelter and safety, which they were
unable to maintain for themselves on the fertile plains of
central France. The investigations of archæologists lead to
the conclusion that the Aquitanians were perhaps the last
population in Europe to adopt the use of metals, and to give
up the employment of tools formed of stone and horn. Such
relics are very abundant in their country at the present day,
and even attracted the notice of Roman writers. The Basque
name for a hatchet is the "lifted stone," *i.e.*, stone set in a
handle; and for a knife, the "edged stone." This slow
advance in material arts may possibly be connected with
their conquest by Gallic tribes, but had ceased long before
the days of Cæsar, who particularly mentions their unrivalled
skill in the art of mining.

Gallia Belgica was occupied by the Belgæ, the most
warlike of the tribes of Gaul. Their territory extended from
the lower Seine to the Rhine, but the southern frontier is
not easily defined, as it crosses the courses of many rivers.
A line drawn from the junction of the Oise and Seine to the
junction of the Moselle and Rhine, but dipping southwards
so as to embrace the valley of the Aisne, and the central
portion of the valley of the Marne, best describes their limits.
  The chief Belgian tribes were the Remi (*Rheims*), the Suessiones (*Soissons*), the Bellovăci (*Beauvais*), the Ambiani
(*Amiens*), the Atrebătes (*Arras*), the Nervians (nearly co-

extensive with the modern Belgium), the Morĭni (*Calais*),* the Menapians, on the marshy estuaries of the Scheldt and Rhine. Besides these there were in the valley of the Meuse several tribes, called the German tribes, of whom the Eburones were the chief, and deserve mention both for their resistance to Rome and for their cruel fate.

Of these tribes the Nervians were the best representatives of the Belgian stock; they were true sons of the soil, wild, passionate, and fierce; and their courage, in the cause of their ancestral independence, knew no fear. They had never come in contact with Rome, whose merchants and enervating luxuries were forbidden access to their borders; for the wine of the south was almost as dangerous and irresistible a temptation to the native Gaul, as the "fire-water," so wickedly supplied by English traders, is to the Red Indian of to-day. The Belgian tribes had in the previous generation successfully repelled the Cimbrians from their country, and consequently, at the time of Cæsar's entry into Gaul, possessed a reputation for courage superior to that of the Celts. During the campaigns of Cæsar this reputation was maintained, for the Nervians were the only single tribe of Gaul who ever threatened Cæsar's army with annihilation, and their incredible bravery is recorded by Cæsar in remarkable words; "*Therefore let none consider that an unreasoning courage which led these brave men to cross a broad river, ascend a steep bank, and fight on most dangerous ground. Courage such as theirs made great difficulties easy.*"

Only those Belgic tribes which approached the borders of Celtic Gaul had important towns; the Remi had Durocortorum and Bibrax; the Bellovaci, Bratuspantium; the Ambiani, Samarobrīva; the Suessiones, Noviodunum; and the Atrebates, Nemetocenna. Eastward of this Cæsar mentions

---

* Extremique hominum Morini. Virg. Æn. viii. 727.

no town except the "fortress of the Aduatuci," which had an exceptional history, and was rather a place of defence than of habitation.

The race to which the Belgians belonged is a question which cannot be determined with certainty. The Remi informed Cæsar that the majority of the Belgian tribes were of German origin, and had crossed the Rhine in early times; Tacitus* says that the Trevers and Nervians of his time eagerly asserted their German descent, and indignantly denied that they were related by blood to the more effeminate Gauls. The Eburones and three others were called together the German tribes, and the Aduatuci, who fought along with the Belgians, were descendants of the Cimbrians and Teutons. These circumstances prove that among the Belgian tribes there was a perceptible admixture of Germanic blood, and lead to the inference that all the Belgians were originally tribes of Germanic race, who had entered Gaul at a date very remote even in Cæsar's time, and so far mingled with the Celtic population whom they conquered as to adopt their language and dress, as well as to a certain degree their civilized habits. The opposite view is that they were true Gauls, undegenerated by defeat or by contact with any foreign influence. In support of this is the argument that they at least used the Celtic language; Morini, the men by the sea; Samarobriva, the bridge of the Samara; Nemetocenna, the sanctuary; are all Celtic words. A stronger argument is that the character displayed by the Belgians in their contest with Cæsar is not German; both in its strength and in its weakness it is Celtic to the core. The enthusiasm with which they took up the enterprise, and the weakness with which they collapsed at the first blow; their thoughtlessness

---

* Germ. c. 28. *Treveri et Nervii circa affectationem Germanicæ originis ultro ambitiosi sunt, tamquam per hanc gloriam sanguinis a similitudine et inertia Gallorum separentur.*

of the future, and inability to work in concert; the supreme vanity and self-absorption of the Bellovaci, as well as the fearless courage and self-sacrifice of the Nervians, are all qualities of the Celt evinced in a high degree. The Germans who were opposed to Cæsar showed military qualities of a very high order, which contrast strongly with the action of the majority of the Belgian tribes. Still the difference between the Belgians and the Celtic Gauls was great, and prevented a hearty co-operation in the insurrection of the year 52; and in our opinion the balance of argument is in favour of the surmise that the Belgians were of Germanic origin. If they were, their position in Gaul finds a parallel in the Franks and other German tribes, who entered Gaul in the decadence of Roman power, and settling there adopted the language and the traditions, together with much of the national character of the people whom they had conquered.

Gallia Celtica, or Celtic Gaul, by far the largest and most important of the three divisions, was inhabited by the true and undoubted Gauls or Celts; they occupied the whole country, from Switzerland to Brest, and it is they who truly represent the Celtic race and name. The names of the chief Celtic tribes are often preserved in the names of the modern towns of France, and should early be familiar to the student of Cæsar. They may be thus named; in the basin of the Rhone, the Helvetii (*Switzerland*), the Sequani (*Besançon*), the Allobrogians (in the Roman Province). In the basin of the Garonne, the Ruteni, the Cadurci (*Cahors*), the Nitio-brŏges, the Bituriges-Vivisci (*Bordeaux*), and the Petrocorii (*Périgord*). On the Charente, the Santones (*Saintonge*). In the Loire basin, the Arverni (*Auvergne*), the Bituriges (*Bourges*), the Lemovices (*Limoges*), the Pictones (*Poitou*); and on the right bank, the Æduans (near *Autun*), the Car-nutes (*Orleans*), the Turones (*Tours*), the Andes (*Angers*), the Namnetes (*Nantes*). In Normandy and Brittany, the

Aulerci (*Evreux*), the Redones (*Rennes*), the Venĕti (*Vannes*), the Osismi (*Brest*), the Venelli (*Manche*), and other tribes called the Aremorican tribes, from two Celtic words meaning "beside the sea." In the basin of the Seine, the Lingones (*Langres*), the Mandubii, the Senones (*Sens*), the Parisii (*Paris*). At the sources of the Meuse, the Leuci; and on the Moselle, the Mediomatrĭci (*Metz*), and the Treveri (*Tréves*).

The country was thickly populated, and had many cities, surrounded by walls, whose structure excited the admiration of Cæsar both on account of the beauty and the utility of the fabric. The chief of these cities were; Bibracte (*Mont Beuvray*), Cabillōnum (*Châlons-sur-Saône*), Matisco (*Macon*), and Noviodunum (*Nevers*), among the Æduans; Vesontio (*Besançon*), of the Sequani; Gergovia (near *Clermont-Ferrand*), of the Arverni; Avaricum (*Bourges*), of the Bituriges; besides this the Bituriges had at least twenty walled towns; Lemonum (*Poitiers*), of the Pictones; Genabum (*Orleans*), of the Carnutes; Alesia (*Alise St. Reine*), of the Mandubii; Agedincum (*Sens*), of the Senones; Andematunnum (*Langres*), of the Lingones. It is difficult to estimate the number of the population; the Helvetians alone were 368,000; the Aduatuci, a small Belgian tribe, were at least 57,000; the Nervians were 240,000. Calculations based on the number of men called out to bear arms in the campaign against the Belgians estimate the number of the Belgic population at 2,000,000. Celtic Gaul was more thickly populated than Belgium, where much of the land was covered with marshes and virgin forests, and, as it contains nearly four times the extent of Belgic territory, its population may be roughly reckoned at 8,000,000.

The Celtic people were advanced in material civilization, for they had to a large extent developed the resources of their wealthy country. The conception that they were a "barbarous" nation, in the sense that the aborigines of Australia

or the Red Indians of North America are barbarous popula-
tions, must, if it exists, be at once dismissed from the mind.
On the contrary, they were an important branch of the Indo-
Germanic stock, who had brought with them from their
Asiatic home, and developed to a certain extent in their
European settlements, the same ideas of religion, of individual
liberty, and of political relations, as have been the common
inheritance of all the progressive nations of Europe.

Agriculture was extensively practised, and with such
method, that in the chalk districts the exhausted ground was
repaired with dressings of chalk marl, a custom which excited
the admiration of Roman farmers, and is practised at the
present day. Sheep and cattle were a more fertile source of
revenue, as the land of central France is adapted by nature for
pasturage, and the *Gallica pascua* already brought profit to
Roman traders. They had also learned to turn to account
the mineral resources of their country. Cornwall had for
many centuries been famous for its tin mines, and the bars
of British tin, required in the European markets for the
manufacture of bronze—for bronze is an alloy of copper and
tin—all passed through Gallic hands. Thus from an early
date the Gauls were expert workers in bronze; in Cæsar's
time they worked this metal largely for brooches, rings and
torques, and generally for ornamental purposes, not for
weapons of war or for domestic tools, in the manufacture of
which iron had long superseded the softer and more expensive
bronze. Iron was worked in Aquitania and in Auvergne,
where the workmen of St. Etienne and Le Creusot of to-day
are the lineal descendants of the miners of Cæsar's time;
doubtless, considering the general distribution of this metal
in nature, and the extent to which it was used in Gaul, it
was also produced at other local centres.

The Gauls were also expert workers in gold, though they
did not possess this metal in abundance. They learned from
the Massiliots the art of coinage, about the date 250 B.C., but

limited themselves almost entirely to copying the dies upon Greek coins. This faculty of imitation and of the adoption of useful arts is mentioned by Cæsar as one of the national characteristics. "*They are a race*," he says, "*of great cleverness, and of great ability in imitating everything, and of doing anything that they are taught by any one.*" The gold which they possessed was chiefly used in ornaments, armlets and torques worn round the neck, the decoration of a chief.

In the art of shipbuilding the Gauls were in advance of their time. The tribes of Brittany, especially the Veneti, had constructed sailing vessels so large and stout, and so high out of the water, that they could fearlessly sail upon the ocean, leaving behind the water near the coast, the only portion of the sea open to the Roman mariner. The use both of timber and of iron, and the peculiar sails of leather in these vessels, excited Cæsar's admiration; for his own ships of war were puny beside the heavy hulls of the 'barbarian' craft. The Veneti in their ocean-going fleet possessed a power which might have anticipated the results of modern commerce and knowledge by many a century, and their annihilation by Cæsar is one of the most cruel tales in the annals of war.

The Celts had learned the use of letters from the Greeks of Marseilles, just as in earlier years the Romans had acquired the same knowledge from the Greeks of Cumæ; private accounts and state registers were kept in writing, and a few inscriptions still remain, where the language is Celtic and the letters are Greek.

In population, material wealth, and adventurous courage, the Gauls were fairly matched with their Roman foe; it is their political and social relations which betray a weak and disorganized society, and were the true reason of their subjection to Roman power. Each tribe possessed political independence, and made war and peace on its own responsibility. Tribes were partially united by leagues, of which the

Arvernian and the Æduan leagues were so important that
their rival claims divided every tribe and every household in
Celtic Gaul. "*Not merely in every state and every district and
subdivision of a state, but almost in every household there are
two parties.*" These words are Cæsar's first observation on
the state of Gaul, and prove how impressive the fact appeared
to him. The Arvernians were the national party ; in the years
122 and 121 B.C. they had borne the brunt of battle with the
Romans in the Rhone valley, while the Æduans had asked
for Roman aid, and proudly submitted to being called the
friends and brothers of Rome. Thus the tribe or clan was a
unit, and the league or party was a unit, but the nation or
race was not a unit ; it was divided like a dichotomous plant,
in which every part of the living growth, from the stem to
the smallest leaflet, is parted in two. Slowly, as one by one
Cæsar conquered the various tribes, the consciousness that
they were one in race, manners, and religion, and should also
be united in political feeling and action, arose and spread
fast, like the touch of fire, from centre to centre of the
susceptible race. This faith, the possibility of national unity,
inspired and sustained the brief career of Vercingetorix, and
created for a moment the union which he desired. It was
too late ; his object was generally accepted, but the principles
of warfare, which that object made necessary, were slowly
recognized, and to the last he was disloyally supported ; not
even in the cause of freedom, nor at the call of every Celtic
community, could the Æduan forget his rivalry, and submit
to the orders of an Arvernian.

The government of the various tribes was in the hands of
a privileged class, which consisted of knights or nobles, and
of priests or Druids. Both were essentially castes ; the knights
monopolized control of political and military relations, while
in religious, legal, and social affairs the Druids were supreme.
"*The general population,*" to use Cæsar's words, "*was in the
position of slaves.*" In a few tribes the ancient office of king

remained, but it was a survival, and the king was commonly
an old man.   It seems to have been only in the generation
previous to Cæsar that the royal government fell into disuse;
it is probable that in the terrible times of the Cimbrian and
Teuton invasion the monarchic government had proved
quite unable to meet the crisis, and had at once fallen into
discredit.   Its disappearance was a loss to the national
cause, as the rule of ambitious and factious nobles, and the
retinues which they kept to ensure their influence, fostered
the tendencies to disunion and disintegration. When the royal
office was abolished, power fell into the hands of the council
of elders, a body which was entirely swayed by the more
powerful or more turbulent knights or nobles.   It is true
that a magistrate was appointed, possessing, like the Roman
consuls, authority only for a year.   Among the Æduans, and
perhaps elsewhere, he was named the " *Vergobreth*," or
" worker of judgment." This officer's power was strangely
circumscribed by the lawlessness of powerful chiefs.   Orgetorix came before the Helvetian magistrate with a retinue of ten
thousand men, and defied his authority.   Among the Æduans,
Liscus and Divitiacus, the chief magistrate and one of the chief
Druids, were unable, without support from Roman arms,
to stand against the unofficial influence of Dumnorix.   There
is no instance throughout the Gallic war where the magistrate
appears as a person whose office or authority is respected.
The power of the law was so absolutely overthrown that the
majority of the population had no security except in the
" following" of some great lord.   Sinking under the burden
of debt or of taxation, many of the humbler sort voluntarily
accepted servitude with the great and powerful.

The knight or noble was the most characteristic representative of Celtic life, and it is the more necessary to conceive
in some degree his general position and character, as the
opponents to Cæsar could only come from the knightly class.
The Celtic knight lived by arms, and was turbulent and

ambitious. His sole source of power and influence consisted in the number of vassals and clients whom he could bring into the field. If he succeeded in obtaining not merely a large following of men, but also an accumulation of money sufficient to ensure the support of his followers, he became a power in the community with which the law could not cope. Dumnorix, the Æduan, was such a chief; birth, ability, retinue, wealth, all united to form his power. The ambition which had won so much could not rest, but its further objects were ill-defined. His first design, according to Cæsar, was, by supporting the Helvetians in their migration, to embroil Celtic Gaul in confusion and warfare. Out of this confusion the Æduans, Sequans, and Helvetians, firmly leagued together, would issue victorious, and establish a supremacy over Celtic Gaul. The presence of Cæsar baulked such an enterprise; hence Dumnorix at once became the enemy of Cæsar. Yet his opposition seems to have arisen because his individual ambition was thwarted, and not because the independence of Gaul was endangered, so that he does not yet deserve to be named the champion of the national cause. How far his views altered during the four ensuing years of his life it is impossible to know; his opposition to the Roman influence did not alter, and it is probable that he shared in the growing conception of Celtic nationality, and was organizing a widespread and more truly national resistance to Roman arms, when he was cut down by the sword of Cæsar's centurion.

The retinue of such a chief were soldiers, not civilians, although they lived in cities; almost their only employment was war, and they were rarely without employment. Where the retinue was so large, there must have been various degrees of rank; Cæsar mentions two, *ambacti* or vassals, and *clientes* or dependents. In all ranks the virtue of the Gallic warrior was devotion to his chief; indeed self-sacrifice was so natural to Gallic feeling that the custom seems to have been general* for every chief to have a body-guard of knights who were under a vow to share life and death with their leader. Among the Aquitanian tribes this guard sometimes numbered six hundred men, who were named " *soldurii.*" Cæsar asserts that no case was known where a soldurian had failed, on the death of his leader in battle, to keep his vow at the price of his life.

Side by side with the knights were the Druids, or priestly class, who had great power and influence. They presided at all sacrifices, both national and domestic; they were interpreters of omens, a vast power, amid a superstitious people; they were the permanent legal court of the country, deciding on murders, inheritances, and disputed boundaries. They could inflict the severest of all social penalties by refusing to grant to the offender a share in the privileges of religion. In the case of an interregnum they exercised the duties of the chief magistrate. They were in fact the custodians of learning, mythology, religion, and law; they paid no taxes, and were free from military service; plainly their influence was respected, and they had a thoroughly national position. Their authority was recognized throughout all Gaul, so that they formed a uniting bond in the divided country. Little as we know of them, we know that they did not absolutely fall short of this high position. Cæsar tells us that the chief doctrine which they inculcated was the immortality of the soul, and the chief practical consequence which they drew from the belief was that, since there is no annihilation of the soul, men should fight for their country, and scorn the fear of death. Thus fearlessness and self-sacrifice, the ennobling moral qualities of the Celtic nation, were also hallowed by the blessing and by the hopes of

---

* Litaviccus, a minor Æduan chief, was attended by a body of *clientes, quibus more Gallorum nefas est etiam in extrema fortuna deserere patronos.*

religion. In the great rising under Vercingetorix against the Roman arms, it is evident that the Druids had much to do with the organization of the conspiracy. It was among the Carnutes, in whose land was the most sacred place of the Druids, that the meetings were held, and the oaths were sworn, in pursuance of which it was resolved to make a desperate fight for national independence. The Druids are popularly known only in connection with the cruel human sacrifices which they practised; but, in spite of these hideous superstitious rites, it must be allowed that they did not altogether lose sight of their national position and duties.

The military organization of the Celts showed the weakness of their political constitution. The knights formed the flower of the army, and the foot-soldiers, although personally courageous, were not trained to the profession of arms. They had no military engines, they had not the skill to choose the right position for an encampment, nor the patience to fortify their positions by strong entrenchments. Their reckless courage and devoted self-sacrifice, though it twice excites the admiration of so impassive a narrator as Cæsar, was no match for the elaborate military tactics of a Roman army, especially when these tactics were under the control of a consummate master of the military art. Their weakness was most thoroughly seen by their greatest soldier, Vercingetorix, who in his great attempt endeavoured not to fight the Romans, but to starve them. Elated by success he deserted this policy, in an evil hour for the independence of Gaul.

The Germans.—Tradition pointed backwards to a time when the Celtic nation was not only mistress of the Rhine, but sent forth detachments to the eastward, who drove out the previous occupants, and formed settlements upon German soil. These days were long since past; the Gauls had long been confessedly inferior to the Germans, both in infantry and in cavalry manœuvres. It was therefore an act of

suicidal folly, when, about the year 72 B.C., the Sequans and
the Arvernians, in their contest for supremacy with the
Æduans, asked help from Ariovistus, a leader of the *Suebian*
bands, a name which has already been explained to mean
the advanced guard of various German tribes. The assistance
had been successfully given, but, at the time of Cæsar's
entrance into Gaul, the heavy price which had to be paid was
proving intolerable. The Sequans had been forced to sur-
render a third of their lands, and bodies of Germans, number-
ing about 100,000 fighting men, were already settled on the
left bank of the Rhine between Strasburg and Mühlhausen.
The pass of Belfort, which is the natural highway from
Germany into France, and which was so gallantly maintained
by the French in the war of 1870-71, was already in German
hands. The tribes which had crossed over were the Triboci,
the Nemetes, and the Vangiones.

BOOK I.

———✦———

ARGUMENT.

I.—*Preface.*

    c. 1. The land and inhabitants of Gaul described.

II.—*The Helvetian War.*

    cc. 2-4. Orgetorix persuades the Helvetians to leave their homes and find new settlements in Celtic Gaul; his secret designs, and death. cc. 5-11. The Helvetians, attempting to force a passage through the Roman Province, are prevented by the strength of Cæsar's defensive works. They enter Gaul by the narrow passage between Mount Jura and the Rhone. The Æduans, and other tribes under Roman protection, appeal to Cæsar for assistance. c. 12. Cæsar surprises and annihilates the Tigurini. cc. 13-14. Divico's embassy and Cæsar's reply. c. 15. Defeat of Cæsar's cavalry by the Helvetians. cc. 16-20. Cæsar appeals to the Æduan chiefs, Divitiacus and Liscus, to supply his army with provisions. Liscus, the Vergobreth, or chief magistrate, informs Cæsar that Dumnorix, the brother of Divitiacus, is using his influence to prevent supplies being forwarded. Cæsar designs to execute Dumnorix, but is prevented by the entreaties of Divitiacus. cc. 21-22. The mistake of P. Considius. cc. 23-29. Battle with the Helvetians. They are defeated, and the remnant, with the exception of the Boians, forced to return to their original abodes.

III.—*The War with Ariovistus.*

cc. 30-33. The chiefs of Celtic Gaul, after holding a council, ask Cæsar to defend them against Ariovistus, a German king, who has conquered them, and is depriving them of their lands. Cæsar undertakes to check the aggressions of the German chief; his reasons. cc. 34-36. He sends envoys to Ariovistus, asking for an interview, which is refused; a second embassy is answered with defiance. cc. 37-38. Cæsar advances and occupies Vesontio, cc. 39-41, where the army is seized by a universal panic. Cæsar's speech to his officers. Order is restored, and the army marches forward into the Rhine valley. cc. 42-46. Cæsar's interview with Ariovistus broken off by the German cavalry attacking the Roman legionaries. c. 47. Two Gauls, sent as envoys by Cæsar, are thrown into chains by Ariovistus. c. 48. Manœuvres of the German cavalry. cc. 49-50. Ariovistus assaults Cæsar's lesser camp, but fears to accept a general engagement before the new moon. cc. 51-54. Cæsar forces a battle, and gains a signal victory. The Germans are driven across the Rhine; the Suebian bands retire; the army is led into winter quarters, and Cæsar starts for Hither Gaul to hold his proconsular courts.

These events occurred in the year 58 B.C.

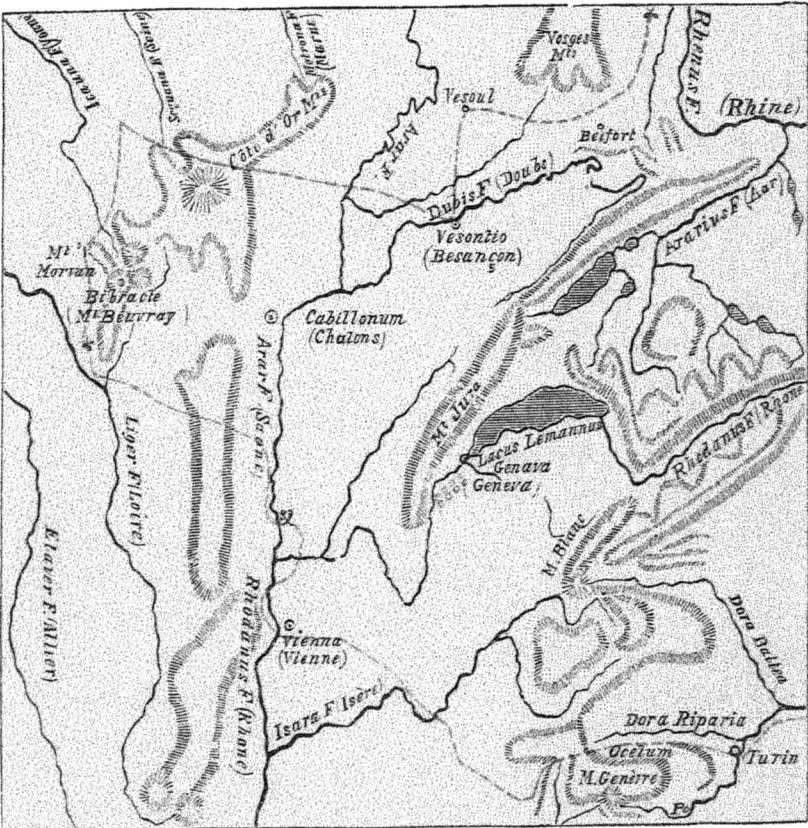

Map labels: Iscara F.(Isere), Caraus M. Sornis, Matrona F.(Marne), Vesges Mts, Rhenus F., Côte d'Or Mts, Vesoul, Arar F., Beifort, (Rhine), Dubis F.(Doube), Vesontio (Besançon), Arariuz F.(Aar), Mt. Morvan, Bibracte (Mt. Beuvray), Cabillonum (Chalons), Arar F.(Saône), Mt. Jura, Lacus Lemannus, Genava (Geneva), Rhodanus F.(Rhone), Liger F.(Loire), Mt. Rhone, Dora Baltea, Elaver F.(Allier), Rhodanus F.(Rhone), Vienna (Vienne), Isara F.(Isere), Dora Riparia, Ocelum, M.Genèvre, Turin, Po

C. JULII CÆSARIS

DE

BELLO GALLICO.

LIBER PRIMUS.

I. Gallia est omnis divisa in partes tres, quarum unam 1 incolunt Belgae, aliam Aquitani, tertiam, qui ipsorum lingua Celtae, nostra Galli appellantur. Hi omnes lingua, institutis, 2 legibus inter se differunt. Gallos ab Aquitanis Garumna flumen, a Belgis Matrona et Sequana dividit. Horum omnium 3 fortissimi sunt Belgae, propterea quod a cultu atque humanitate provinciae longissime absunt, minimeque ad eos mercatores saepe commeant atque ea, quae ad effeminandos animos pertinent, important, proximique sunt Germanis, qui trans Rhenum incolunt, quibuscum continenter bellum gerunt. Qua de causa Helvetii quoque reliquos Gallos virtute praece- 4 dunt, quod fere cotidianis proeliis cum Germanis contendunt, cum aut suis finibus eos prohibent, aut ipsi in eorum finibus bellum gerunt. Eorum una pars, quam Gallos obtinere 5 dictum est, initium capit a flumine Rhodano; continetur Garumna flumine, Oceano, finibus Belgarum ; attingit etiam ab Sequanis et Helvetiis flumen Rhenum; vergit ad septentriones. Belgae ab extremis Galliae finibus oriuntur ; 6 pertinent ad inferiorem partem fluminis Rheni ; spectant in septentrionem et orientem solem. Aquitania a Garumna 7

flumine ad Pyrenaeos montes et ad eam partem Oceani, quae
est ad Hispaniam, pertinet; spectat inter occasum solis et
septentriones.

1   II.   Apud Helvetios longe nobilissimus et ditissimus fuit
Orgetorix.   Is M. Messala et M. Pisone consulibus regni
cupiditate inductus coniurationem nobilitatis fecit et civitati
persuasit, ut de finibus suis cum omnibus copiis exirent :
2 *perfacile esse, cum virtute omnibus praestarent, totius Galliae*
3 *imperio potiri.*   Id hoc facilius eis persuasit, quod undique
loci natura Helvetii continentur : una ex parte flumine Rheno,
latissimo atque altissimo, qui agrum Helvetium a Germanis
dividit ; altera ex parte monte Iura altissimo, qui est inter
Sequanos et Helvetios ; tertia lacu Lemanno et flumine Rho-
4 dano, qui provinciam nostram ab Helvetiis dividit.   His rebus
fiebat, ut et minus late vagarentur, et minus facile finitimis
bellum inferre possent ; qua ex parte homines bellandi cupidi
5 magno dolore afficiebantur.   Pro multitudine autem hominum
et pro gloria belli atque fortitudinis angustos se finis habere
arbitrabantur, qui in longitudinem milia passuum ducenta
quadraginta, in latitudinem centum octoginta patebant.

1   III.   His rebus adducti et auctoritate Orgetorigis permoti
constituerunt ea, quae ad proficiscendum pertinerent, com-
parare, iumentorum et carrorum quam maximum numerum
coëmere, sementes quam maximas facere, ut in itinere copia
frumenti suppeteret, cum proximis civitatibus pacem et
2 amicitiam confirmare.   Ad eas res conficiendas biennium
sibi satis esse duxerunt : in tertium annum profectionem lege
3 confirmant.   Ad eas res conficiendas Orgetorix deligitur.   Is
4 sibi legationem ad civitates suscepit.   In eo itinere persuadet
Castico, Catamantaloedis filio, Sequano, cuius pater regnum
in Sequanis multos annos obtinuerat et a senatu populi
Romani amicus appellatus erat, ut regnum in civitate sua
5 occuparet, quod pater ante habuerat; itemque Dumnorigi
Aeduo, fratri Divitiaci, qui eo tempore principatum in civitate
obtinebat ac maxime plebi acceptus erat, ut idem conaretur,

persuadet eique filiam suam in matrimonium dat. *Perfacile* 6 *factu esse* illis probat *conata perficere, propterea quod ipse suae civitatis imperium oltenturus esset : non esse dubium, quin totius Galliae plurimum Helvetii possent ; se suis copiis suoque exercitu illis regna conciliaturum* confirmat. Hac oratione 7 adducti inter se fidem et iusiurandum dant et regno occupato per tres potentissimos ac firmissimos populos totius Galliae sese potiri posse sperant. Ea res est Helvetiis per indicium enuntiata.

IV. Moribus suis Orgetorigem ex vinclis causam dicere 1 coëgerunt ; damnatum poenam sequi oportebat, ut igni cremaretur. Die constituta causae dictionis Orgetorix ad 2 iudicium omnem suam familiam, ad hominum milia decem, undique coëgit et omnes clientes obaeratosque suos, quorum magnum numerum habebat, eodem conduxit : per eos, ne causam diceret, se eripuit. Cum civitas ob eam rem incitata 3 armis ius suum exsequi conaretur, multitudinemque hominum ex agris magistratus cogerent, Orgetorix mortuus est ; neque 4 abest suspicio, ut Helvetii arbitrantur, quin ipse sibi mortem consciverit.

V. Post eius mortem nihilo minus Helvetii id, quod con- 1 stituerant, facere conantur, ut e finibus suis exeant. Ubi 2 iam se ad eam rem paratos esse arbitrati sunt, oppida sua omnia, numero ad duodecim, vicos ad quadringen- tos, reliqua privata aedificia incendunt, frumentum omne, praeterquam quod secum portaturi erant, comburunt, ut domum reditionis spe sublata paratiores ad omnia pericula subeunda essent, trium mensum molita cibaria sibi quemque domo efferre iubent. Persuadent Rauricis et Tulingis et 3 Latovicis finitimis, uti eodem usi consilio oppidis suis vicisque exustis una cum iis proficiscantur, Boiosque, qui trans Rhenum incoluerant et in agrum Noricum transierant Noreiamque oppugnarant, receptos ad se socios sibi ad- sciscunt.

VI. Erant omnino itinera duo, quibus itineribus domo 1

4 *

exire possent: unum per Sequanos, angustum et difficile,
inter montem Iuram et flumen Rhodanum, vix qua singuli
carri ducerentur; mons autem altissimus impendebat, ut
facile perpauci prohibere possent: alterum per provinciam
nostram, multo facilius atque expeditius, propterea quod
inter fines Helvetiorum et Allobrogum, qui nuper pacati
erant, Rhodanus fluit, isque nonnullis locis vado transitur.
2 Extremum oppidum Allobrogum est proximumque Helvetiorum finibus Genava. Ex eo oppido pons ad Helvetios
3 pertinet. Allobrogibus sese vel persuasuros, quod nondum bono animo in populum Romanum viderentur, existimabant, vel vi coacturos, ut per suos fines eos ire
4 paterentur. Omnibus rebus ad profectionem comparatis
diem dicunt, qua die ad ripam Rhodani omnes conveniant.
Is dies erat a. d. V. Kal. Apr. L. Pisone, A. Gabinio
consulibus.

1   VII.   Caesari cum id nuntiatum esset, eos per provinciam
nostram iter facere conari, maturat ab urbe proficisci et
quam maximis potest itineribus in Galliam ulteriorem
2 contendit et ad Genavam pervenit. Provinciae toti quam
maximum potest militum numerum imperat (erat omnino
in Gallia ulteriore legio una), pontem, qui erat ad Gena-
3 vam, iubet rescindi.   Ubi de eius adventu Helvetii cer-
tiores facti sunt, legatos ad eum mittunt nobilissimos
civitatis, cuius legationis Nammeius et Verucloetius principem locum obtinebant, qui dicerent *sibi esse in animo sine
ullo maleficio iter per provinciam facere, propterea quod aliud
iter haberent nullum : rogare, ut eius voluntate id sibi facere*
4 *liceat.*   Caesar, quod memoria tenebat L. Cassium consulem
occisum exercitumque eius ab Helvetiis pulsum et sub
iugum missum, concedendum non putabat; neque homines
inimico animo data facultate per provinciam itineris
faciendi temperaturos ab iniuria et maleficio existimabat.
5 Tamen, ut spatium intercedere posset, dum milites, quos
imperaverat, convenirent, legatis respondit *diem se ad delibe-*

randum sumpturum: si quid vellent, ad Idus Apr. reverterentur.

VIII.   Interea ea legione, quam secum habebat, militi- ı
busque, qui ex provincia convenerant, a lacu Lemanno, qui
in flumen Rhodanum influit, ad montem Iuram, qui fines
Sequanorum ·ab Helvetiis dividit, milia passuum decem
novem murum in altitudinem pedum sedecim fossamque
perducit.   Eo opere perfecto praesidia disponit, castella 2
communit, quo facilius, si se invito transire conarentur,
prohibere possit.   Ubi ea dies, quam constituerat cum 3
legatis, venit, et legati ad eum reverterunt, negat, *se more
et exemplo populi Romani posse iter ulli per provinciam
dare, et, si vim facere conentur, prohibiturum* ostendit.
Helvetii ea spe deiecti navibus iunctis ratibusque com- 4
pluribus factis, alii vadis Rhodani, qua minima altitudo
fluminis erat, nonnumquam interdiu, saepius noctu, si
perrumpere possent, conati operis munitione et militum
concursu et telis repulsi hoc conatu destiterunt.

IX.   Relinquebatur una per Sequanos via, qua Sequanis ı
invitis propter angustias ıre non poterant.   His cum sua 2
sponte persuadere non possent, legatos ad Dumnorigem
Aeduum mittunt, ut eo deprecatore a Sequanis impetrarent.   Dumnorix gratia et largitione apud Sequanos pluri- 3
mum poterat et Helvetiis erat amicus, quod ex ea civitate
Orgetorigis filiam in matrimonium duxerat, et cupiditate
regni adductus novis rebus studebat et quam plurimas
civitates suo beneficio habere obstrictas volebat.   Itaque 4
rem suscipit et a Sequanis impetrat, ut per fines suos
Helvetios ire patiantur, obsidesque uti inter sese dent,
perficit: Sequani, ne itinere Helvetios prohibeant, Helvetii, ut sine maleficio et iniuria transeant.

X.   Caesari renuntiatur, Helvetiis esse in animo, per ı
agrum Sequanorum et Aeduorum iter in Santonum fines
facere, qui non longe a Tolosatium finibus absunt, quae
civitas est in provincia.   Id si fieret, intellegebat magno cum 2

periculo provinciae futurum, ut homines bellicosos, populi
Romani inimicos, locis patentibus maximeque frumenta-
3 riis finitimos haberet.   Ob eas causas ei munitioni, quam
fecerat, T. Labienum legatum praefecit; ipse in Italiam
magnis itineribus contendit duasque ibi legiones conscribit et tres, quae circum Aquileiam hiemabant, ex hibernis
educit et, qua proximum iter in ulteriorem Galliam per
4 Alpes erat, cum his quinque legionibus ire contendit.   Ibi
Ceutrones et Graioceli et Caturiges locis superioribus
5 occupatis itinere exercitum prohibere conantur.   Compluribus his proeliis pulsis ab Ocelo, quod est citerioris
provinciae extremum, in fines Vocontiorum ulterioris provinciae die septimo pervenit; inde in Allobrogum fines,
ab Allobrogibus in Segusiavos exercitum ducit.   Hi sunt
extra provinciam trans Rhodanum primi.

1   XI.   Helvetii iam per angustias et fines Sequanorum suas
copias traduxerant et in Aeduorum fines pervenerant
2 eorumque agros populabantur.   Aedui, cum se suaque
ab iis defendere non possent, legatos ad Caesarem mittunt
rogatum auxilium : *Ita se omni tempore de populo Romano
meritos esse, ut paene in conspectu exercitus nostri agri vastari,
liberi eorum in servitutem abduci, oppida expugnari non
3 debuerint.*   Eodem tempore Aedui Ambarri, necessarii et
consanguinei Aeduorum, Caesarem certiorem faciunt sese
depopulatis agris non facile ab oppidis vim hostium pro-
4 hibere.   Item Allobroges, qui trans Rhodanum vicos posses-
sionesque habebant, fuga se ad Caesarem recipiunt et demon-
5 strant sibi praeter agri solum nihil esse reliqui.   Quibus
rebus adductus Caesar non exspectandum sibi statuit, dum
omnibus fortunis sociorum consumptis in Santonos Helvetii
pervenirent.

1   XII.   Flumen est Arar, quod per fines Aeduorum et
Sequanorum in Rhodanum influit incredibili lenitate, ita
ut oculis, in utram partem fluat, iudicari non possit.   Id
2 Helvetii ratibus ac lintribus iunctis transibant.   Ubi per

exploratores Caesar certior factus est, tres iam copiarum partes Helvetios id flumen traduxisse, quartam fere partem citra flumen Ararim reliquam esse, ¡de tertia vigilia cum legionibus tribus e castris profectus ¡ad eam partem pervenit, ¡ quae nondum flumen transierat. Eos impeditos 3 et inopinantes aggressus magnam eorum partem concidit · reliqui fugae sese mandarunt atque in proximas silvas abdiderunt. Is pagus appellabatur Tigurinus; nam omnis 4 civitas Helvetia in quattuor pagos divisa est. Hic pagus unus, cum domo exisset patrum nostrorum memoria, L. Cassium consulem interfecerat et eius exercitum sub iugum miserat. Ita sive casu sive consilio deorum im- 5 mortalium, quae pars civitatis Helvetiae insignem calamitatem populo Romano intulerat, •ea princeps poenas persolvit. Qua in re Caesar non solum publicas, sed etiam 6 privatas iniurias ultus est, quod eius soceri L. Pisonis avum, L. Pisonem legatum, Tigurini eodem proelio, quo Cassium, interfecerant.

XIII. Hoc proelio facto reliquas copias Helvetiorum ut 1 consequi posset, pontem in Arare faciendum curat atque ita exercitum traducit. Helvetii(repentino eius adventu com- 2 moti)[cum id, (quod ipsi diebus viginti aegerrime confecerant) {ut flumen transirent} illum uno die fecisse intellegerent,] legatos ad eum mittunt; cuius legationis Divico princeps fuit, qui bello Cassiano dux Helvetiorum fuerat. Is ita cum Caesare egit: *Si pacem populus Romanus cum 3 Helvetiis faceret, in eam partem ituros atque ibi futuros Helvetios, ubi eos Caesar constituisset atque esse voluisset; sin bello persequi perseveraret, reminisceretur et veteris incommodi populi Romani et pristinae virtutis Helvetiorum. Quod improviso unum pagum adortus esset, cum ii, qui 4 flumen transissent, suis auxilium ferre non possent, ne ob eam rem aut suae magnopere virtuti tribueret aut ipsos despiceret. Se ita a patribus maioribusque suis didicisse, ut magis virtute 5 contenderent, quam dolo aut insidiis niterentur. Quare ne 6 committeret, ut is locus, ubi constitissent, ex calamitate populi Romani et internecione exercitus nomen caperet aut memoriam proderet.*

1   XIV.   His Caesar ita respondit : *Eo sibi minus dubitationis dari, quod eas res, quas legati Helvetii commemorassent, memoria teneret, atque eo gravius ferre, quo minus merito populi Romani accidissent : qui si alicuius iniuriae sibi conscius fuisset, non fuisse difficile cavere ; sed eo deceptum, quod neque commissum a se intellegeret, quare timeret, neque*
2 *sine causa timendum putaret.   Quod si veteris contumeliae oblivisci vellet, num etiam recentium iniuriarum, quod eo invito iter per provinciam per vim temptassent, quod Aeduos, quod Ambarros, quod Allobrogas vexassent, memoriam deponere*
3 *posse ?   Quod sua victoria tam insolenter gloriarentur, quodque tam diu se impune iniurias tulisse admirarentur, eodem pertinere ; consuesse enim deos immortales, quo gravius homines ex commutatione rerum doleant, quos pro scelere eorum ulcisci velint, his secundiores interdum res et diuturniorem impuni-*
4 *tatem concedere.   Cum ea ita sint, tamen, si obsides ab iis sibi dentur, uti ea, quae polliceantur, facturos intellegat, et si Aeduis de iniuriis, quas ipsis sociisque eorum, intulerint, item si Allobrogibus satisfaciant, sese cum iis pacem esse facturum.*
5 Divico respondit : *Ita Helvetios a maioribus suis institutos esse, uti obsides accipere, non dare, consuerint : eius rei populum Romanum esse testem.*   Hoc responso dato discessit.

1   XV.   Postero die castra ex eo loco movent.   Idem facit Caesar equitatumque omnem, ad numerum quattuor milium, quem ex omni provincia et Aeduis atque eorum sociis coactum habebat, praemittit, qui videant, quas in partes
2 hostes iter faciant.   Qui cupidius novissimum agmen insecuti alieno loco cum equitatu Helvetiorum proelium
3 committunt ; et pauci de nostris cadunt.   Quo proelio sublati Helvetii, quod quingentis equitibus tantam multitudinem equitum propulerant, audacius subsistere nonnumquam et novissimo agmine proelio nostros lacessere coe

perunt. Caesar suos a proelio continebat ac satis habebat 4
in praesentia hostem rapinis, pabulationibus populationi-
busque prohibere. Ita dies circiter quindecim iter fece- 5
runt, uti inter novissimum hostium agmen et nostrum
primum non amplius quinis aut senis milibus passuum
interesset.

XVI. Interim cotidie Caesar Aeduos frumentum, quod 1
essent publice polliciti, flagitare. Nam propter frigora, 2
quod Gallia sub septentrionibus, ut ante dictum est, posita
est, non modo frumenta in agris matura non erant, sed ne
pabuli quidem satis magna copia suppetebat: eo autem
frumento, quod flumine Arare navibus subvexerat, propterea
minus uti poterat, quod iter ab Arare Helvetii averterant,
a quibus discedere nolebat. Diem ex die ducere Aedui: 3
conferri, comportari, adesse dicere. Ubi se diutius duci 4
intellexit et diem instare, quo die frumentum militibus metiri
oporteret, convocatis eorum principibus, quorum magnam
copiam in castris habebat, in his Divitiaco et Lisco, qui
summo magistratui praeerat (quem Vergobretum appellant
Aedui, qui creatur annuus et vitae necisque in suos habet
potestatem), graviter eos accusat, quod, cum neque emi
neque ex agris sumi posset, tam necessario tempore, tam
propinquis hostibus ab iis non sublevetur; praesertim cum
magna ex parte eorum precibus adductus bellum susceperit,
multo etiam gravius, quod sit destitutus, queritur.

XVII. Tum demum Liscus oratione Caesaris adductus, 1
quod antea tacuerat, proponit: *Esse nonnullos, quorum auc-
toritas apud plebem plurimum valeat, qui privatim plus possint,
quam ipsi magistratus. Hos seditiosa atque improba oratione* 2
*multitudinem deterrere, ne frumentum conferant, quod debeant:
praestare, si iam principatum Galliae obtinere non possint,* 3
*Gallorum quam Romanorum imperia perferre, neque dubitare,
quin, si Helvetios superaverint Romani, una cum reliqua Gallia
Aeduis libertatem sint erepturi. Ab eisdem nostra consilia* 4
quaeque in castris gerantur hostibus enuntiari: hos a se coërceri

non posse : quin etiam, quod necessario rem coactus Caesari enuntiarit, intellegere sese, quanto id cum periculo fecerit, et ob eam causam, quam diu potuerit, tacuisse.

1   XVIII. Caesar hac oratione Lisci Dumnorigem, Divitiaci fratrem, designari sentiebat, sed, quod pluribus praesentibus eas res iactari nolebat, celeriter concilium dimittit, Liscum retinet. Quaerit ex solo ea, quae in conventu dixerat. Dicit liberius atque audacius. Eadem secreto ab aliis quaerit;
2 reperit esse vera : *Ipsum esse Dumnorigem, summa audacia, magna apud plebem propter liberalitatem gratia, cupidum rerum novarum. Compluris annos portoria reliquaque omnia Aeduorum vectigalia parvo pretio redempta habere, propterea*
3 *quod illo licente contra liceri audeat nemo. His rebus et suam rem familiarem auxisse et facultates ad largiendum magnas comparasse ; magnum numerum equitatus suo sumptu semper*
4 *alere et circum se habere; neque solum domi, sed etiam apud finitimas civitates largiter posse, atque huius potentiae causa matrem in Biturigibus homini illic nobilissimo ac potentissimo collocasse, ipsum ex Helvetiis uxorem habere, sororem ex matre*
5 *et propinquas suas nuptum in alias civitates collocasse. Favere et cupere Helvetiis propter eam affinitatem, odisse etiam suo nomine Caesarem et Romanos, quod eorum adventu potentia eius deminuta et Divitiacus frater in antiquum locum gratiae atque*
6 *honoris sit restitutus. Si quid accidat Romanis, summam in spem per Helvetios regni obtinendi venire; imperio populi Romani non modo de regno, sed etiam de ea, quam habeat,*
7 *gratia desperare.* Reperiebat etiam in quaerendo Caesar, *quod proelium equestre adversum paucis ante diebus esset factum, initium eius fugae factum a Dumnorige atque eius equitibus* (nam equitatui, quem auxilio Caesari Aedui miserant, Dumnorix praeerat) : *eorum fuga reliquum esse equitatum perterritum.*

1   XIX. Quibus rebus cognitis, cum ad has suspiciones certissimae res accederent, quod per fines Sequanorum Helvetios traduxisset, quod obsides inter eos dandos curasset,

quod ea omnia non modo iniussu suo et civitatis, sed etiam inscientibus ipsis fecisset, quod a magistratu Aeduorum accusaretur, satis esse causae arbitrabatur, quare in eum aut ipse animadverteret, aut civitatem animadvertere iuberet. His omnibus rebus unum repugnabat, quod Divitiaci fratris 2 summum in populum Romanum studium, summam in se voluntatem, egregiam fidem, iustitiam, temperantiam cognoverat : nam, ne eius supplicio Divitiaci animum offenderet, verebatur. Itaque prius, quam quicquam conaretur, Divitia- 3 cum ad se vocari iubet et cotidianis interpretibus remotis per C. Valerium Procillum, principem Galliae provinciae, familiarem suum, cui summam omnium rerum fidem habebat, cum eo colloquitur : simul commonefacit, quae ipso 4 praesente in concilio Gallorum de Dumnorige sint dicta, et ostendit, quae separatim quisque de eo apud se dixerit. Petit atque hortatur, ut sine eius offensione animi vel ipse de 5 eo causa cognita statuat, vel civitatem statuere iubeat.

XX. Divitiacus multis cum lacrimis Caesarem com- 1 plexus obsecrare coepit, ne quid gravius in fratrem statueret : *Scire se illa esse vera, nec quemquam ex eo plus quam se doloris* 2 *capere, propterea quod, cum ipse gratia plurimum domi atque in reliqua Gallia, ille minimum propter adulescentiam posset, per se crevisset ; quibus opibus ac nervis non solum ad minuendam gratiam, sed paene ad perniciem suam uteretur. Sese tamen et amore fraterno et existimatione vulgi commoveri. Quod si quid ei a Caesare gravius accidisset, cum ipse eum* 3 *locum amicitiae apud eum teneret, neminem existimaturum, non sua voluntate factum ; qua ex re futurum, uti totius Galliae animi a se averterentur.* Haec cum pluribus verbis flens a 4 Caesare peteret, Caesar eius dextram prendit ; consolatus rogat, finem orandi faciat ; tanti eius apud se gratiam esse ostendit, uti et reipublicae iniuriam et suum dolorem eius voluntati ac precibus condonet. Dumnorigem ad se vocat, 5 fratrem adhibet ; quae in eo reprehendat, ostendit, quae ipse intellegat, quae civitas queratur, proponit ; monet, ut in

reliquum tempus omnes suspiciones vitet; praeterita se
Divitiaco fratri condonare dicit. Dumnorigi custodes ponit,
ut, quae agat, quibuscum loquatur, scire possit.

ɪ   XXI. Eodem die ab exploratoribus certior factus hostes
sub monte consedisse milia passuum ab ipsius castris octo,
qualis esset natura montis et qualis in circuitu ascensus, qui
2 cognoscerent, misit. Renuntiatum est, facilem esse. De
tertia vigilia Titum Labienum, legatum pro praetore, cum
duabus legionibus et iis ducibus, qui iter cognoverant, summum iugum montis ascendere iubet; quid sui consilii sit,
3 ostendit. Ipse de quarta vigilia eodem itinere, quo hostes
ierant, ad eos contendit equitatumque omnem ante se mittit.
4 P. Considius, qui rei militaris peritissimus habebatur et in
exercitu L. Sullae et postea in M. Crassi fuerat, cum exploratoribus praemittitur.

ɪ   XXII. Prima luce, cum summus mons a T. Labieno
teneretur, ipse ab hostium castris non longius mille et quingentis passibus abesset, neque, ut postea ex captivis comperit,
aut ipsius adventus aut Labieni cognitus esset, Considius
equo admisso ad eum accurrit, dicit montem, quem a
Labieno occupari voluerit, ab hostibus teneri: *id se a*
2 *Gallicis armis atque insignibus cognovisse.* Caesar suas
copias in proximum collem subducit, aciem instruit. Labienus, ut erat ei praeceptum a Caesare, ne proelium committeret, nisi ipsius copiae prope hostium castra visae essent,
ut undique uno tempore in hostes impetus fieret, monte
3 occupato nostros exspectabat proelioque abstinebat. Multo
denique die per exploratores Caesar cognovit et montem a
suis teneri et Helvetios castra movisse et Considium timore
perterritum, quod non vidisset, pro viso sibi renuntiasse. Eo
die quo consuerat intervallo hostes sequitur et milia passuum
tria ab eorum castris castra ponit.

ɪ   XXIII. Postridie eius diei, quod omnino biduum
supererat, cum exercitui frumentum metiri oporteret, et quod
a Bibracte, oppido Aeduorum longe maximo et copiosissimo,

nonamplius milibus passuum octodecim aberat, rei frumentariae prospiciendum existimavit : iter ab Helvetiis avertit
ac Bibracte ire contendit. Ea res per fugitivos L. Aemilii, 2
decurionis equitum Gallorum, hostibus nuntiatur. Helvetii, 3
seu quod timore perterritos Romanos discedere a se existimarent, eo magis, quod pridie superioribus locis occupatis
proelium non commisissent, sive eo, quod re frumentaria
intercludi posse confiderent, commutato consilio atque itinere
converso nostros a novissimo agmine insequi ac lacessere
coeperunt.

XXIV.   Postquam id animum advertit, copias suas Cæsar 1
in proximum collem subducit equitatumque, qui sustineret
hostium impetum, misit.   Ipse interim in colle medio tri- 2
plicem aciem instruxit legionum quattuor veteranarum ; sed in
summo iugo duas legiones, quas in Gallia citeriore proxime
conscripserat, et omnia auxilia collocari ac totum montem
hominibus compleri, et interea sarcinas in unum locum conferri et eum ab his, qui in superiore acie constiterant, muniri
iussit.   Helvetii cum omnibus suis carris secuti impedimenta 3
in unum locum contulerunt ; ipsi confertissima acie reiecto
nostro equitatu phalange facta sub primam nostram aciem
successerunt.

XXV.   Caesar primum suo, deinde omnium ex conspectu 1
remotis equis, ut aequato omnium periculo spem fugae
tolleret, cohortatus suos proelium commisit.   Milites e loco 2
superiore pilis missis facile hostium phalangem perfregerunt.
Ea disiecta gladiis destrictis in eos impetum fecerunt.   Gallis 3
magno ad pugnam erat impedimento, quod pluribus eorum
scutis uno ictu pilorum transfixis et colligatis, cum ferrum
se inflexisset, neque evellere neque sinistra impedita satis
commode pugnare poterant, multi ut diu iactato brachio
praeoptarent scutum manu emittere et nudo corpore pugnare.
Tandem vulneribus defessi et pedem referre et, quod mons 4
suberat circiter mille passuum *spatio,* eo se recipere coeperunt.
Capto monte et succedentibus nostris Boii et Tulingi, 5

qui hominum milibus circiter quindecim agmen hostium
claudebant et novissimis praesidio erant, ex itinere nostros
latere aperto aggressi circumvenire, et id conspicati Helvetii,
qui in montem sese receperant, rursus instare et proelium
6 redintegrare coeperunt. Romani conversa signa bipartito
intulerunt: prima ac secunda acies, ut victis ac summotis
resisteret, tertia, ut venientes sustineret.

1 XXVI. Ita ancipiti proelio diu atque acriter pugnatum
est. Diutius cum sustinere nostrorum impetus non possent,
alteri se, ut coeperant, in montem receperunt, alteri ad
2 impedimenta et carros suos se contulerunt. Nam hoc toto
proelio, cum ab hora septima ad vesperum pugnatum sit,
3 aversum hostem videre nemo potuit. Ad multam noctem
etiam ad impedimenta pugnatum est, propterea quod pro
vallo carros obiecerant et e loco superiore in nostros
venientes tela coniciebant et nonnulli inter carros rotasque
mataras ac tragulas subiciebant nostrosque vulnerabant.
4 Diu cum esset pugnatum, impedimentis castrisque nostri
potiti sunt. Ibi Orgetorigis filia atque unus e filiis captus est.
5 Ex eo proelio circiter milia hominum centum triginta super-
fuerunt eaque tota nocte continenter ierunt: nullam partem
noctis itinere intermisso in fines Lingonum die quarto pervenerunt, cum et propter vulnera militum et propter sepul-
turam occisorum nostri triduum morati eos sequi non
6 potuissent. Caesar ad Lingonas litteras nuntiosque misit,
ne eos frumento neve alia re iuvarent: qui si iuvissent, se eodem
loco, quo Helvetios, habiturum. Ipse triduo intermisso cum
omnibus copiis eos sequi coepit.

1 XXVII. Helvetii omnium rerum inopia adducti legatos
de deditione ad eum miserunt. Qui cum eum in itinere
convenissent seque ad pedes proiecissent suppliciterque locuti
flentes pacem petissent, atque eos in eo loco, quo tum essent,
2 suum adventum exspectare iussisset, paruerunt. Eo postquam Caesar pervenit, obsides, arma, servos, qui ad eos
3 perfugissent, poposcit. Dum ea conquiruntur et conferuntur

nocte intermissa, circiter hominum milia sex eius pagi, qui
Verbigenus appellatur, sive timore perterriti, ne armis traditis
supplicio afficerentur, sive spe salutis inducti, quod in tanta
multitudine dediticiorum suam fugam aut occultari, aut
omnino ignorari posse existimarent, prima nocte e castris
Helvetiorum egressi ad Rhenum finesque Germanorum
contenderunt.

XXVIII. Quod ubi Caesar resciit, quorum per fines 1
ierant, his, uti conquirerent et reducerent, si sibi purgati esse
vellent, imperavit : reductos in hostium numero habuit ;
reliquos omnes obsidibus, armis, perfugis traditis in dedi-
tionem accepit. Helvetios, Tulingos, Latovicos in fines suos, 2
unde erant profecti, reverti iussit, et quod omnibus frugibus
amissis domi nihil erat, quo famem tolerarent, Allobrogibus
imperavit, ut iis frumenti copiam facerent : ipsos oppida
vicosque, quos incenderant, restituere iussit. Id ea maxime 3
ratione fecit, quod noluit eum locum, unde Helvetii disces-
serant, vacare, ne propter bonitatem agrorum Germani, qui
trans Rhenum incolunt, e suis finibus in Helvetiorum fines
transirent et finitimi Galliae provinciae Allobrogibusque
essent. Boios, petentibus Aeduis, quod egregia virtute 4
erant cogniti, ut in finibus suis collocarent, concessit ; quibus
illi agros dederunt, quosque postea in parem iuris libertatisque
condicionem, atque ipsi erant, receperunt.

XXIX. In castris Helvetiorum tabulae repertae sunt 1
litteris Graecis confectae et ad Caesarem relatae, quibus in
tabulis nominatim ratio confecta erat, qui numerus domo
exisset eorum, qui arma ferre possent, et item separatim pueri,
senes mulieresque. Quarum omnium rerum summa erat 2
capitum Helvetiorum milia cclxiii, Tulingorum milia xxxvi,
Latovicorum xiiii, Rauricorum xxiii, Boiorum xxxii ;
ex his, qui arma ferre possent, ad milia xcii. Summa
omnium fuerunt ad milia ccclxviii. Eorum, qui domum 3
redierunt, censu habito, ut Caesar imperaverat, repertus est
numerus milium c et x.

1   XXX. Bello Helvetiorum confecto totius fere Galliae legati, principes civitatum, ad Caesarem gratulatum convenerunt : *Intellegere sese, tametsi pro veteribus Helvetiorum iniuriis populi Romani ab his poenas bello repetisset, tamen eam rem non minus ex usu terrae Galliae quam populi Romani accidisse, propterea quod eo consilio florentissimis rebus domos suas Helvetii reliquissent, uti toti Galliae bellum inferrent imperioque potirentur locumque domicilio ex magna copia deligerent, quem ex omni Gallia opportunissimum ac fructuosissimum iudicassent, reliquasque civitates stipendiarias haberent.*

2 Petierunt, *uti sibi concilium totius Galliae in diem certam indicere idque Caesaris voluntate facere liceret : sese habere quasdam res, quas ex communi consensu ab eo petere vellent.*

3 Ea re permissa diem concilio constituerunt et iureiurando, ne quis enuntiaret, nisi quibus communi consilio mandatum esset, inter se sanxerunt.

1   XXXI. Eo concilio dimisso idem principes civitatum, qui ante fuerant, ad Caesarem reverterunt petieruntque, uti sibi secreto de sua omniumque salute cum eo agere liceret.

2 Ea re impetrata sese omnes flentes Caesari ad pedes proiecerunt : *Non minus se id contendere et laborare, ne ea, quae dixissent, enuntiarentur, quam uti ea, quae vellent, impetrarent, propterea quod, si enuntiatum esset, summum in cruciatum se*

3 *venturos viderent.* Locutus est pro his Divitiacus Aeduus : *Galliae totius factiones esse duas : harum alterius principatum tenere Aeduos, alterius Arvernos. Hi cum tantopere de potentatu inter se multos annos contenderent, factum esse, uti ab Arvernis*

4 *Sequanisque Germani mercede arcesserentur. Horum primo circiter milia quindecim Rhenum transisse : posteaquam agros et cultum et copias Gallorum homines feri ac barbari adamassent, traductos plures : nunc esse in Gallia ad centum et viginti milium numerum. Cum his Aeduos eorumque clientes semel atque iterum armis contendisse ; magnam calamitatem pulsos accepisse, omnem nobilitatem, omnem senatum, omnem equitatum*

5 *amisisse. Quibus proeliis calamitatibusque fractos, qui et sua*

*virtute et populi Romani hospitio atque amicitia plurimum ante
in Gallia potuissent, coactos esse Sequanis obsides dare nobilissimos civitatis, et iureiurando civitatem obstringere, sese neque
obsides repetituros neque auxilium a populo Romano imploratu-
ros neque recusaturos, quo minus perpetuo sub illorum dicione
atque imperio essent. Unum se esse ex omni civitate Aeduorum,* 6
*qui adduci non potuerit, ut iuraret aut liberos suos obsides daret.
Ob eam rem se ex civitate profugisse et Romam ad senatum
venisse auxilium postulatum, quod solus neque iureiurando
neque obsidibus teneretur. Sed peius victoribus Sequanis quam* 7
*Aeduis victis accidisse, propterea quod Ariovistus, rex Germano-
rum, in eorum finibus consedisset tertiamque partem agri
Sequani, qui esset optimus totius Galliae, occupavisset et nunc
de altera parte tertia Sequanos decedere iuberet, propterea quod
paucis mensibus ante Harudum milia hominum viginti quattuor
ad eum venissent, quibus locus ac sedes pararentur. Futurum* 8
*esse paucis annis, uti omnes ex Galliae finibus pellerentur atque
omnes Germani Rhenum transirent: neque enim conferendum
esse Gallicum cum Germanorum agro, neque hanc consuetudinem victus cum illa comparandam. Ariovistum autem, ut* 9
*semel Gallorum copias proelio vicerit, quod proelium factum sit
Admagetobrigae, superbe et crudeliter imperare, obsides nobilis-
simi cuiusque liberos poscere et in eos omnia exempla cruciatusque
edere, si qua res non ad nutum aut ad voluntatem eius facta sit.
Hominem esse barbarum, iracundum, temerarium; non posse* 10
eius imperia diutius sustinere. Nisi si quid in Caesare 11
*populoque Romano sit auxilii, omnibus Gallis idem esse facien-
dum, quod Helvetii fecerint, ut domo emigrent, aliud domicilium,
alias sedes remotas a Germanis petant fortunamque, quaecumque accidat, experiantur. Haec si enuntiata Ariovisto sint,* 12
*non dubitare, quin de omnibus obsidibus, qui apud eum sint,
gravissimum supplicium sumat. Caesarem vel auctoritate sua* 13
*atque exercitus, vel recenti victoria, vel nomine populi Romani
deterrere posse, ne maior multitudo Germanorum Rhenum tradu-
catur, Galliamque omnem ab Ariovisti iniuria posse defendere.*

1　XXXII.　Hac oratione ab Divitiaco habita omnes, qui aderant, magno fletu auxilium a Caesare petere coeperunt. Animadvertit Caesar unos ex omnibus Sequanos nihil earum rerum facere, quas ceteri facerent, sed tristes capite demisso 2 terram intueri.　Eius rei causa quae esset, miratus ex ipsis quaesiit.　Nihil Sequani respondere, sed in eadem tristitia taciti permanere.　Cum ab his saepius quaereret neque ullam omnino vocem exprimere posset, idem Divitiacus Aeduus 3 respondit: *Hoc esse miseriorem gravioremque fortunam Sequanorum prae reliquorum, quod soli ne in occulto quidem neque auxilium implorare auderent absentisque Ariovisti crudelitatem, velut si coram adesset, horrerent, propterea quod reliquis tamen fugae facultas daretur, Sequanis vero, qui intra fines suos Ariovistum recepissent, quorum oppida omnia in potestate eius essent, omnes cruciatus essent perferendi.*

1　XXXIII.　His rebus cognitis Caesar Gallorum animos verbis confirmavit pollicitusque est *sibi eam rem curae futuram : magnam se habere spem et beneficio suo et auctoritate* 2 *adductum Ariovistum finem iniuriis facturum.*　Hac oratione habita concilium dimisit.　Et secundum ea multae res eum hortabantur, quare sibi eam rem cogitandam et suscipiendam putaret, imprimis quod Aeduos, fratres consanguineosque saepenumero a senatu appellatos, in servitute atque in dicione videbat Germanorum teneri eorumque obsides esse apud Ariovistum ac Sequanos intellegebat; quod in tanto imperio populi Romani turpissimum sibi et reipublicae 3 esse arbitrabatur.　Paulatim autem Germanos consuescere Rhenum transire et in Galliam magnam eorum multitudinem venire populo Romano periculosum videbat, neque sibi homines feros ac barbaros temperaturos existimabat, quin, cum omnem Galliam occupavissent, ut ante Cimbri Teutonique fecissent, in provinciam exirent atque inde in Italiam contenderent, praesertim cum Sequanos a provincia nostra Rhodanus divideret; quibus rebus quam maturrime occur- 4 rendum putabat.　Ipse autem Ariovistus tantos sibi spiritus, tantam arrogantiam sumpserat, ut ferendus non videretur.

XXXIV. Quamobrem placuit ei, ut ad Ariovistum legatos 1 mitteret, qui ab eo postularent, uti aliquem locum medium utriusque colloquio diceret : *Velle sese de republica et summis utriusque rebus cum eo agere.* Ei legationi Ariovistus respondit: 2 *Si quid ipsi a Caesare opus esset, sese ad eum venturum fuisse; si quid ille se velit, illum ad se venire oportere. Praeterea se* 3 *neque sine exercitu in eas partes Galliae venire audere, quas Caesar possideret, neque exercitum sine magno commeatu atque molimento in unum locum contrahere posse; sibi autem mirum videri, quid in sua Gallia, quam bello vicisset, aut Caesari aut omnino populo Romano negotii esset.*

XXXV. His responsis ad Caesarem relatis iterum ad 1 eum Caesar legatos cum his mandatis mittit : *Quoniam tanto suo populique Romani beneficio affectus, cum in consulatu suo rex atque amicus a senatu appellatus esset, hanc sibi populoque Romano gratiam referret, ut in colloquium venire invitatus gravaretur neque de communi re dicendum sibi et cognoscendum putaret, haec esse, quae ab eo postularet : primum, ne quam* 2 *hominum multitudinem amplius trans Rhenum in Galliam traduceret; deinde obsides, quos haberet ab Aeduis, redderet Sequanisque permitteret, ut, quos illi haberent, voluntate eius reddere illis liceret ; neve Aeduos iniuria lacesseret, neve his sociisve eorum bellum inferret. Si id ita fecisset, sibi populoque* 3 *Romano perpetuam gratiam atque amicitiam cum eo futuram : si non impetraret, sese, quoniam M. Messala, M. Pisone consulibus senatus censuisset, uti, quicumque Galliam provinciam obtineret, quod commodo reipublicae facere posset, Aeduos ceterosque amicos populi Romani defenderet, sese Aeduorum iniurias non neglecturum.*

XXXVI. Ad haec Ariovistus respondit: *Jus esse belli, ut,* 1 *qui vicissent, iis, quos vicissent, quemadmodum vellent, imperarent: item populum Romanum victis non ad alterius praescriptum, sed ad suum arbitrium imperare consuesse. Si* 2

5 *

ipse populo Romano non praescriberet, quemadmodum suo iure uteretur, non oportere sese a populo Romano in suo iure
3 *impediri. Aeduos sibi, quoniam belli fortunam temptassent et armis congressi ac superati essent, stipendiarios esse factos. Magnam Caesarem iniuriam facere, qui suo adventu vectigalia*
4 *sibi deteriora faceret. Aeduis se obsides redditurum non esse, neque iis neque eorum sociis iniuria bellum illaturum, si in eo manerent, quod convenissent, stipendiumque quotannis penderent; si id non fecissent, longe iis fraternum nomen populi Romani*
5 *ajuturum. Quod sibi Caesar denuntiaret se Aeduorum iniurias non neglecturum, neminem secum sine sua pernicie contendisse. Cum vellet, congrederetur: intellecturum, quid invicti Germani, exercitatissimi in armis, qui inter annos quatuordecim tectum non subissent, virtute possent.*

1 XXXVII. Haec eodem tempore Caesari mandata referebantur et legati ab Aeduis et a Treveris veniebant: Aedui questum, quod Harudes, qui nuper in Galliam transportati essent, fines eorum popularentur: sese ne obsidibus quidem
2 datis pacem Ariovisti redimere potuisse; Treveri autem, pagos centum Sueborum ad ripas Rheni consedisse, qui Rhenum transire conarentur; his praeesse Nasuam et Cim-
3 berium fratres. Quibus rebus Caesar vehementer commotus maturandum sibi existimavit, ne, si nova manus Sueborum cum veteribus copiis Ariovisti sese coniunxisset, minus facile
4 resisti posset. Itaque re frumentaria quam celerrime potuit comparata magnis itineribus ad Ariovistum contendit.

1 XXXVIII. Cum tridui viam processisset, nuntiatum est ei Ariovistum cum suis omnibus copiis ad occupandum Vesontionem, quod est oppidum maximum Sequanorum
2 contendere triduique viam e suis finibus profecisse. Id ne accideret, magnopere sibi praecavendum Caesar existimabat; namque omnium rerum, quae ad bellum usui erant, summa erat in eo oppido facultas, idque natura loci sic muniebatur, ut magnam ad ducendum bellum daret facultatem, propterea quod flumen Dubis ut circino circumductum paene totum

oppidum cingit; reliquum spatium, quod est non amplius 3 pedum *mille* sexcentorum, qua flumen intermittit, mons continet magna altitudine, ita ut radices montis ex utraque parte ripae fluminis contingant. Hunc murus circumdatus arcem 4 efficit et cum oppido coniungit. Huc Caesar magnis nocturnis diurnisque itineribus contendit occupatoque oppido ibi praesidium collocat.

XXXIX. Dum paucos dies ad Vesontionem rei frumen- 1 tariae commeatusque causa moratur, ex percontatione nostrorum vocibusque Gallorum ac mercatorum, qui ingenti magnitudine corporum Germanos, incredibili virtute atque exercitatione in armis esse praedicabant (*saepenumero sese cum his congressos ne vultum quidem atque aciem oculorum* dicebant *ferre potuisse*), tantus subito timor omnem exercitum occupavit, ut non mediocriter omnium mentes animosque perturbaret. Hic primum ortus est a tribunis 2 militum, praefectis reliquisque, qui ex urbe amicitiae causa Caesarem secuti non magnum in re militari usum habebant · quorum alius alia causa illata, quam sibi ad proficiscendum necessariam esse diceret, petebat, ut eius voluntate discedere liceret; nonnulli pudore adducti, ut timoris suspicionem vitarent, remanebant. Hi neque vultum 3 fingere neque interdum lacrimas tenere poterant; abditi in tabernaculis aut suum fatum querebantur, aut cum familiaribus suis commune periculum miserabantur. Volgo totis castris testamenta obsignabantur. Horum vocibus 4 ac timore paulatim etiam ii, qui magnum in castris usum habebant, milites centurionesque quique equitatui praeerant, perturbabantur. Qui se ex his minus timidos existimari 5 volebant, non se hostem vereri, sed angustias itineris, magnitudinem silvarum, quae intercederent inter ipsos atque Ariovistum, aut rem frumentariam, ut satis commode supportari posset, timere dicebant. Nonnulli etiam Caesari 6 nuntiarant, cum castra moveri ac signa ferri iussisset, non fore dicto audientes milites neque propter timorem signa laturos.

1 XL. Haec cum animadvertisset, convocato consilio omniumque ordinum ad id consilium adhibitis centurionibus vehementer eos incusavit: *Primum, quod, aut quam in partem aut quo consilio ducerentur, sibi quaerendum aut cogitan-* 2 *dum putarent. Ariovistum se consule cupidissime populi Romani amicitiam appetisse: cur hunc tam temere quisquam ab officio* 3 *discessurum iudicaret? Sibi quidem persuaderi cognitis suis postulatis atque aequitate condicionum perspecta eum neque suam neque populi Romani gratiam repudiaturum.* 4 *Quod si furore atque amentia impulsus bellum intulisset, quid tandem vererentur? aut cur de sua virtute aut de* 5 *ipsius diligentia desperarent? Factum eius hostis periculum patrum nostrorum memoria, cum Cimbris et Teutonis a Gaio Mario pulsis non minorem laudem exercitus quam ipse imperator meritus videbatur; factum etiam nuper in Italia servili tumultu, quos tamen aliquid usus ac disciplina, quae a* 6 *nobis accepissent, sublevarent; ex quo iudicari posse, quantum haberet in se boni constantia, propterea quod, quos aliquamdiu inermos sine causa timuissent, hos postea armatos ac victores* 7 *superassent. Denique hos esse eosdem, quibuscum saepenumero Helvetii congressi non solum in suis, sed etiam in illorum finibus plerumque superarint, qui tamen pares esse nostro* 8 *exercitui non potuerint. Si quos adversum proelium et fuga Gallorum commoveret, hos, si quaererent, reperire posse diuturnitate belli defatigatis Gallis Ariovistum, cum multos menses castris se ac paludibus tenuisset neque sui potestatem fecisset, desperantes iam de pugna et dispersos subito adortum* 9 *magis ratione et consilio quam virtute vicisse. Cui rationi contra homines barbaros atque imperitos locus fuisset, hac ne* 10 *ipsum quidem sperare nostros exercitus capi posse. Qui suum timorem in rei frumentariae simulationem angustiasque itineris conferrent, facere arroganter, cum aut de officio imperatoris* 11 *desperare aut praescribere viderentur. Haec sibi esse curae; frumentum Sequanos, Leucos, Lingones subministrare, iamque esse in agris frumenta matura; de itinere ipsos brevi tempore*

iudicaturos. Quod non fore dicto audientes milites neque signa 12
laturi dicantur, nihil se ea re commoveri ; scire enim, quibus-
cumque exercitus dicto audiens non fuerit, aut male re gesta
fortunam defuisse, aut aliquo facinore comperto avaritiam esse
convictam. Suam innocentiam perpetua vita, felicitatem Hel-
vetiorum bello esse perspectam. Itaque se, quod in longiorem 13
diem collaturus fuisset, repraesentaturum et proxima nocte de
quarta vigilia castra moturum, ut quam primum intelligere
posset, utrum apud eos pudor atque officium, an timor valeret.
Quod si praeterea nemo sequatur, tamen se cum sola decima 14
legione iturum, de qua non dubitaret, sibique eam praetoriam
cohortem futuram. Huic legioni Caesar et indulserat praecipue
et propter virtutem confidebat maxime.

XLI. Hac oratione habita mirum in modum conversae 1
sunt omnium mentes, summaque alacritas et cupiditas belli
gerendi innata est, princepsque decima legio per tribunos
militum ei gratias egit, quod de se optimum iudicium fecisset,
seque esse ad bellum gerendum paratissimam confirmavit.
Deinde reliquae legiones per tribunos militum et primorum 2
ordinum centuriones egerunt, uti Caesari satisfacerent. *Se*
neque umquam dubitasse neque timuisse neque de summa belli
suum iudicium, sed imperatoris esse, existimavisse. Eorum 3
satisfactione accepta et itinere exquisito per Divitiacum, quod
ex aliis ei maximam fidem habebat, ut milium amplius quinquaginta circuitu locis apertis exercitum duceret, de quarta
vigilia, ut dixerat, profectus est. Septimo die, cum iter non 4
intermitteret, ab exploratoribus certior factus est, Ariovisti
copias a nostris milibus passuum quattuor et viginti abesse.

XLII. Cognito Caesaris adventu Ariovistus legatos ad 1
eum mittit : *Quod antea de colloquio postulasset, id per se fieri*
licere, quoniam propius accessisset, seque id sine periculo facere
posse existimare. Non respuit condicionem Caesar iamque 2
eum ad sanitatem reverti arbitrabatur, cum id, quod antea
petenti denegasset, ultro polliceretur, magnamque in spem
veniebat, pro suis tantis populique Romani in eum beneficiis

3 cognitis suis postulatis fore, uti pertinacia desisteret. Dies colloquio dictus est ex eo die quintus. Interim saepe ultro citroque cum legati inter eos mitterentur, Ariovistus postulavit, ne quem peditem ad colloquium Caesar adduceret: *Vereri se, ne per insidias ab eo circumveniretur: uterque cum* 4 *equitatu veniret: alia ratione se non esse venturum.* Caesar, quod neque colloquium interposita causa tolli volebat, neque salutem suam Gallorum equitatui committere audebat, commodissimum esse statuit omnibus equis Gallis equitibus detractis eo legionarios milites legionis decimae, cui quam maxime confidebat, imponere, ut praesidium quam amicissi- 5 mum, si quid opus facto esset, haberet. Quod cum fieret, non irridicule quidam ex militibus decimae legions dixit: *Plus, quam pollicitus esset, Caesarem facere: pollicitum se in cohortis praetoriae loco decimam legionem haliturum ad equum rescribere.*

1 XLIII. Planicies erat magna et in ea tumulus terrenus satis grandis. Hic locus aequo fere spatio ab · castris Ariovisti et Caesaris aberat. Eo, ut erat dictum, ad collo- 2 quium venerunt. Legionem Caesar, quam equis devexerat, passibus ducentis ab eo tumulo constituit. Item equites Ariovisti pari intervallo constiterunt. Ariovistus, ex equis ut colloquerentur et praeter se denos ut ad colloquium 3 adducerent, postulavit. Ubi eo ventum est, Caesar initio orationis sua senatusque in eum beneficia commemoravit, *quod rex appellatus esset a senatu, quod amicus, quod munera amplissime missa; quam rem et paucis contigisse et pro magnis hominum officiis consuesse tribui* docebat; *illum, cum neque aditum neque causam postulandi iustam haberet, beneficio ac liberalitate sua ac senatus ea praemia* 4 *consecutum.* Docebat, etiam, *quam veteres quamque iustae causae necessitudinis ipsis cum Aeduis intercederent, quae senatusconsulta quotiens quamque honorifica in eos facta essent, ut omni tempore totius Galliae principatum Aedui tenuissent,* 5 *prius etiam, quam nostram amicitiam appetissent. Populi*

Romani hanc esse consuetudinem, ut socios atque amicos non modo sui nihil deperdere, sed gratia, dignitate, honore auctiores velit esse: quod vero ad amicitiam populi Romani attulissent, id iis eripi quis pati posset? Postulavit deinde eadem, quae 6 legatis in mandatis dederat, *ne aut Aeduis aut eorum sociis bellum inferret; obsides redderet; si nullam partem Germanorum domum remittere posset, at ne quos amplius Rhenum transire pateretur.*

XLIV. Ariovistus ad postulata Caesaris pauca respondit, 1 de suis virtutibus multa praedicavit : *Transisse Rhenum sese non sua sponte, sed rogatum et arcessitum a Gallis ; non sine magna spe magnisque praemiis domum propinquosque reliquisse; sedes habere in Gallia ab ipsis concessas, obsides ipsorum voluntate datos; stipendium capere iure belli, quod victores victis imponere consuerint. Non sese Gallis, sed Gallos sibi* 2 *bellum intulisse: omnes Galliae civitates ad se oppugnandum venisse ac contra se castra habuisse; eas omnes copias a se uno proelio pulsas ac superatas esse. Si iterum experiri velint, se* 3 *iterum paratum sese decertare; si pace uti velint, iniquum esse de stipendio recusare, quod sua voluntate ad id tempus pependerint. Amicitiam populi Romani sibi ornamento et* 4 *praesidio, non detrimento esse oportere, idque se ea spe petisse. Si per populum Romanum stipendium remittatur et dediticii subtrahantur, non minus libenter sese recusaturum populi Romani amicitiam, quam appetierit. Quod multitudinem* 5 *Germanorum in Galliam traducat, id se sui muniendi, non Galliae impugnandae causa facere; eius rei testimonium esse, quod nisi rogatus non venerit, et quod bellum non intulerit, sed defenderit. Se prius in Galliam venisse, quam populum* 6 *Romanum. Numquam ante hoc tempus exercitum populi Romani Galliae provinciae fines egressum. Quid sibi vellet?* 7 *Cur in suas possessiones veniret? Provinciam suam hanc esse Galliam, sicut illam nostram. Ut ipsi concedi non oporteret, si in nostros fines impetum faceret, sic item nos esse iniquos, qui in suo iure se interpellaremus. Quod fratres a senatu* 8

Aeduos appellatos diceret, non se tam barbarum neque tam imperitum esse rerum, ut non sciret neque bello Allobrogum proximo Aeduos Romanis auxilium tulisse neque ipsos in his contentionibus, quas Aedui secum et cum Sequanis habuissent, 9 *auxilio populi Romani usos esse.* Debere se suspicari simulata Caesarem amicitia, quod exercitum in Gallia habeat, sui oppri- 10 mendi causa habere. *Qui nisi decedat atque exercitum deducat ex his regionibus, sese illum non pro amico, sed hoste habiturum; Quod si eum interfecerit, multis sese nobilibus principibusque populi Romani gratum esse facturum; id se ab ipsis per eorum nuntios compertum habere, quorum omnium gratiam atque* 11 *amicitiam eius morte redimere posset. Quod si discessisset et liberam possessionem Galliae sibi tradidisset, magno se illum praemio remuneraturum et, quaecumque bella geri vellet, sine ullo eius labore et periculo confecturum.*

1 XLV. Multa ab Caesare in eam sententiam dicta sunt, quare negotio desistere non posset, et *neque suam neque populi Romani consuetudinem pati, uti optime merentes socios desereret, neque se iudicare Galliam potius esse Ariovisti quam populi Romani.* 2 *Bello superatos esse Arvernos et Rutenos ab Q. Fabio Maximo, quibus populus Romanus ignovisset neque in provinciam* 3 *redegisset neque stipendium imposuisset. Quod si antiquissimum quodque tempus spectari oporteret, populi Romani iustissimum esse in Gallia imperium; si iudicium senatus observari oporteret, liberam debere esse Galliam, quam bello victam suis legibus uti voluisset.*

1 XLVI. Dum haec in colloquio geruntur, Caesari nuntiatum est, equites Ariovisti propius tumulum accedere et ad nostros 2 adequitare, lapides telaque in nostros conicere. Caesar loquendi finem facit seque ad suos recepit suisque imperavit, 3 ne quod omnino telum in hostes reicerent. Nam etsi sine ullo periculo legionis delectae cum equitatu proelium fore videbat, tamen committendum non putabat, ut pulsis hostibus dici posset eos ab se per fidem in colloquio circumventos. 4 Posteaquam in volgus militum elatum est, qua arrogantia in

colloquio Ariovistus usus omni Gallia Romanis interdixisset, impetumque in nostros eius equites fecissent, eaque res colloquium ut diremisset, multo maior alacritas studiumque pugnandi maius exercitui iniectum est.

XLVII. Biduo post Ariovistus ad Caesarem legatos 1 mittit: *Velle se de his rebus, quae inter eos agi coeptae neque perfectae essent, agere cum eo: uti aut iterum colloquio diem constitueret, aut, si id minus vellet, ex suis legatum aliquem ad se mitteret.* Colloquendi Caesari causa visa non est, et eo 2 magis, quod pridie eius diei Germani retineri non poterant, quin in nostros tela conicerent. Legatum ex suis sese magno cum periculo ad eum missurum et hominibus feris obiecturum existimabat. Commodissimum visum est, 3 Gaium Valerium Procillum, C. Valeri Caburi filium, summa virtute et humanitate adulescentem, cuius pater a Gaio Valerio Flacco civitate donatus erat, et propter fidem et propter linguae Gallicae scientiam, qua multa iam Ariovistus longinqua consuetudine utebatur, et quod in eo peccandi Germanis causa non esset, ad eum mittere, et M. Metium, qui hospitio Ariovisti utebatur. His mandavit, ut, quae diceret 4 Ariovistus, cognoscerent et ad se referrent. Quos cum apud se in castris Ariovistus conspexisset, exercitu suo praesente conclamavit: *Quid ad se venirent? An speculandi causa?* Conantis dicere prohibuit et in catenas coniecit.

XLVIII. Eodem die castra promovit et milibus passuum 1 sex a Caesaris castris sub monte consedit. Postridie eius diei praeter castra Caesaris suas copias traduxit et milibus passuum duobus ultra eum castra fecit eo consilio, uti frumento commeatuque, qui ex Sequanis et Aeduis supportaretur, Caesarem intercluderet. Ex eo die dies continuos 2 quinque Caesar pro castris suas copias produxit et aciem instructam habuit, ut, si vellet Ariovistus proelio contendere, ei potestas non deesset. Ariovistus his omnibus diebus exercitum castris continuit, equestri proelio cotidie contendit. Genus hoc erat pugnae, quo se Germani exercuerant. 3 Equitum milia erant sex, totidem numero pedites velocissimi

ac fortissimi, quos ex omni copia singuli singulos suae salutis
4 causa delegerant. Cum his in proeliis versabantur, ad eos se
equites recipiebant : hi, si quid erat durius, concurrebant : si
qui graviore vulnere accepto equo deciderat, circumsistebant;
si quo erat longius prodeundum aut celerius recipiendum,
tanta erat horum exercitatione celeritas, ut iubis equorum
sublevati cursum adaequarent.

1 XLIX. Ubi eum castris se tenere Caesar intellexit, ne
diutius commeatu prohiberetur, ultra eum locum, quo in loco
Germani consederant, circiter passus sexcentos ab iis, castris
idoneum locum delegit acieque triplici instructa ad eum locum
2 venit. Primam et secundam aciem in armis esse, tertiam
castra munire iussit. Hic locus ab hoste circiter passus
3 sexcentos, uti dictum est, aberat. Eo circiter hominum
numero sedecim milia expedita cum omni equitatu Ariovistus
misit, quae copiae nostros perterrerent et munitione pro-
4 hiberent. Nihilo secius Caesar, ut ante constituerat, duas
acies hostem propulsare, tertiam opus perficere iussit.
Munitis castris duas ibi legiones reliquit et partem auxiliorum,
quattuor reliquas in castra maiora reduxit.

1 L. Proximo die instituto suo' Caesar e castris utrisque
copias suas eduxit paulumque a maioribus castris progressus
aciem instruxit, hostibus pugnandi potestatem fecit. Ubi ne
tum quidem eos prodire intellexit, circiter meridiem exerci-
2 tum in castra reduxit. Tum demum Ariovistus partem
suarum copiarum, quae castra minora oppugnaret, misit.
Acriter utrimque usque ad vesperum pugnatum est. Solis
occasu suas copias Ariovistus multis et inlatis et acceptis
3 vulneribus in castra reduxit. Cum ex captivis quaereret
Caesar, quamobrem Ariovistus proelio non decertaret, hanc
reperiebat causam, quod apud Germanos ea consuetudo esset,
ut matresfamiliae eorum sortibus et vaticinationibus declar-
arent, utrum proelium committi ex usu esset, necne : eas ita
4 dicere : *Non esse fas Germanos superare, si ante novam lunam
proelio contendissent.*

1 LI. Postridie eius diei Caesar praesidio utrisque castris,

quod satis esse visum est, reliquit, omnis alarios in conspectu hostium pro castris minoribus constituit, quod minus multitudine militum legionariorum pro hostium numero valebat, ut ad speciem alariis uteretur; ipse triplici instructa acie usque ad castra hostium accessit. Tum demum 2 necessario Germani suas copias castris eduxerunt generatimque constituerunt paribus intervallis, Harudes, Marcomanos, Triboces, Vangiones, Nemetes, Sedusios, Suebos, omnemque aciem suam redis et carris circumdederunt, ne qua spes in fuga relinqueretur. Eo mulieres imposuerunt, 3 quae in proelium proficiscentes milites passis manibus flentes implorabant, ne se in servitutem Romanis traderent.

LII. Caesar singulis legionibus singulos legatos et 1 quaestorem praefecit, uti eos testes suae quisque virtutis haberet; ipse a dextro cornu, quod eam partem minime firmam hostium esse animadverterat, proelium commisit. Ita 2 nostri acriter in hostes signo dato impetum fecerunt, itaque hostes repente celeriterque procurrerunt, ut spatium pila in hostes coniciendi non daretur. Reiectis pilis, comminus gladiis pugnatum est. At Germani, celeriter ex consuetudine 3 sua phalange facta impetus gladiorum exceperunt. Reperti 4 sunt complures nostri milites, qui in phalangas insilirent et scuta manibus revellerent et desuper vulnerarent. Cum 5 hostium acies a sinistro cornu pulsa atque in fugam conversa esset, a dextro cornu vehementer multitudine suorum nostram aciem premebant. Id cum animadvertisset Publius 6 Crassus adulescens, qui equitatui praeerat, quod expeditior erat quam hi, qui inter aciem versabantur, tertiam aciem laborantibus nostris subsidio misit.

LIII. Ita proelium restitutum est, atque omnes hostes 1 terga verterunt neque prius fugere destiterunt, quam ad flumen Rhenum milia passuum ex eo loco circiter quinque pervenerunt. Ibi perpauci aut viribus confisi tranare con- 2 tenderunt aut lintribus inventis sibi salutem reppererunt. In 3 his fuit Ariovistus, qui naviculam deligatam ad ripam nactus

ea profugit: reliquos omnes consecuti equites nostri inter-
4 fecerunt.   Duae fuerunt Ariovisti uxores, una Sueba natione,
quam domo secum duxerat, altera Norica, regis Voccionis
soror, quam in Gallia duxerat a fratre missam: utraque in
ea fuga periit.   Duae *fuerunt* filiae ; harum altera occisa,
5 altera capta est.   Gaius Valerius Procillus, cum a custodibus
in fuga trinis catenis vinctus traheretur, in ipsum Caesarem
6 hostis equitatu persequentem incidit.   Quae quidem res
Caesari non minorem quam ipsa victoria voluptatem attulit,
quod hominem honestissimum provinciae Galliae, suum
familiarem et hospitem, ereptum e manibus hostium sibi
restitutum videbat, neque eius calamitate de tanta voluptate
7 et gratulatione quicquam fortuna deminuerat.   Is se praesente de se ter sortibus consultum dicebat, utrum igni statim
necaretur, an in aliud tempus reservaretur : sortium beneficio
se esse incolumem.   Item M. Metius repertus et ad eum
reductus est.

1   LIV.   Hoc proelio trans Rhenum nuntiato Suebi, qui ad
ripas Rheni venerant, domum reverti coeperunt ; quos Ubii,
qui proximi Rhenum incolunt, perterritos insecuti, magnum
2 ex his numerum occiderunt.   Caesar una aestate duobus
maximis bellis confectis maturius paulo, quam tempus anni
postulabat, in hiberna in Sequanos exercitum deduxit,
3 hibernis Labienum praeposuit ; ipse in citeriorem Galliam
ad conventus agendos profectus est.

NOTES

CHAPTER I.

'**Gallia omnis.**' "The whole country known as Gaul contains 1 three divisions." *Omnis* is important, as Gallia by itself frequently means the land of Celtic Gaul alone. On the divisions of Gaul, see Introd. p. 18. *Galli* here, as perhaps always, the inhabitants of Celtic Gaul.

'**lingua.**' The Aquitanian language was either Basque or 2 Iberian, which are equivalent terms, or Celtic mixed with Basque; the Belgian probably showed traces of German influence.

'**Belgæ.**' Cæsar, writing as a Roman and hereditary enemy of 3 the Gallic race, at once mentions the most dangerous foe; we could wish he had said more of the " differences in language, civil customs, and laws."

'**cultus et humanitas provinciæ,**' litt. "the mode of life and civilization of our province," better, " the civilized manners of our province." An English adj. and subst. often give the most fitting translation of two Latin substantives. On the Province, see Introd. p. 18.

'**ea quæ—pertinent,**' "those things which tend to weaken courage," *i.e.*, " effeminating luxuries." The Latin n. pl. is represented in English by an abstract substantive, and the relative clause by an adjective.

'**qui, quibuscum.**' No *et* unites these relatives because they are not similar to each other; the first *qui*-clause might be replaced by an adj. agreeing with *Germanis*, and the second *qui* refers to the idea formed by the subst. and adj. together; " the Germans of the right bank of the Rhine, with whom they are perpetually at war."

'**Helvetii.**' The Helvetians lived between the lake of Geneva, 4 Mount Jura, the Rhine, and the lake of Constance. Their tribe was divided into four cantons, of which Cæsar names two, the *Verbigenus* and the *Tigurinus*. They had twelve walled towns, and as many as four hundred village settlements.

'cum prohibent,' "either in driving them out." *Cum*, when, with pres. tense has the indicative.

5 'eorum,' the Gauls as a whole, not the Helvetians. "One of these three divisions."

'dituem est,' "it has been said;" the historic style requires that the narrator should hardly ever mention himself.

'initium capit a' = "begins with."

'obtinere, continetur,' "occupy," "is bounded by." Be careful not to construe *obtineo* I obtain, *contineo* I contain.

'ab Sequanis,' "on the side of the Sequans," cp. *a tergo, a fronte*, &c. The Sequans were a powerful tribe whose lands extended between the Saone, the Rhone, and Mount Jura, and on the Rhine to near Strasburg. Their capital was Vesontio (*Besançon*) on the Dubis (*Doubs*), then, as now, an important fortress on the eastern frontier of Gaul.

'vergit ad sept.' "lies towards the north," *i.e.* of the Roman Province. So Aquitania is N.W. of Narbo, the capital of the Rom. Prov.

The whole of this chapter is introductory. The public of Rome, for whom Cæsar was writing, knew little of the Roman Province of Gaul, and nothing of the country beyond, which had so lately been independent Gaul. To pave the way for more accurate knowledge, Cæsar describes the extensive country, the different populations, the courage of individual tribes, and the threatening proximity of German invaders. His preface may be said to portend a tale of dissensions and intrigue, long marches and bloody conflicts.

CHAPTER II.

1 'Apud Helvetios.' The abruptness and the simplicity of this transition from the preface to the story is a noticeable feature of Cæsar's writing. He copies the style of Epic narration. ἦν δέ τις ἐν Τρώεσσι Δόλων.

'M. Mess. et M. Pis. cons.,' "in the consulate of M. Mess. and M. Piso," 61 B.C., three years previous to the time when Cæsar entered Gaul.

'civitati persuasit,' "persuaded his fellow-countrymen;" *i.e.* procured a vote in the general assembly of all freemen, or *concilium*, which met in arms.

'de finibus exirent.' "to go forth away from their territories;"

i.e. not to return; *exire ex finibus* would be said of a portion forming a settlement and leaving their friends behind. Obs. *exirent* after *civitas.*

'**cum omn. cop.**' "along with their whole population," men, women, and children. Modern history knows of no spectacle similar to the emigration of the Helvetii, which Cæsar is about to describe.

'**praestarent,**' with a dative. Livy uses it with an accusative. 2 *quantum Galli virtute ceteros mortales praestarent.* B. 5. c. 36.

'**undique nat. loci cont.**' = "are hemmed in on every side by 3 the natural features of the country."

'**qua ex parte**' = "from which side," *i.e.* "from these con- 4 siderations," or reflections.

'**dolore,**' *dolor* is not 'grief,' but the 'sting of pain' either to the body or, as here, to the mind. The clause may be translated, "reflections which rankled bitterly in the minds of the warlike people."

'**pro multitudine,**' "in proportion to their population;" stated 5 in c. 29 at 368,000, of which a fourth, 92,000, is calculated as the number of fighting men.

'**milia passuum.**' The Roman mile of one thousand paces was 1618 English yards in length, 142 yards short of the English mile. According to our mode of reckoning, the Roman *passus* was two paces; it was measured from the heel of the foot as it was lifted from the ground in walking to the heel of the same foot when it next touched the ground; the distance was five Roman feet.

The breadth of Switzerland from Basle to the St. Gotthard is exactly eighty Roman miles, the length from Genèva to Lake Constance is only two hundred miles. Either Cæsar made a mistake, —and he had no personal knowledge of the country, — or he included in Helvetian territory the lands of the Latovices and Tulingi, beyond the Rhine, who joined in the migration.

CHAPTER III.

'**adducti**'="induced," "led on." '**permoti**'="thoroughly stirred," 1 "decided." **inductus** in c. 2 is "blinded," "misled."

'**auctoritate**' = "personal influence" of an individual, not the authority of a magistrate, which, if civil, is *potestas*, if military, *imperium.*

'**ea quae pertinerent,**' "the necessaries required for." *pertinerent* subjunctive because it forms a part of the resolution of the Helvetians.

'**lege,**' "by a decree of the assembled nation." The deliberate 2 purpose shown both in the preparations made and in the formalities observed is very remarkable.

3 '**Ad eas res conficiendas.**' Two sentences begin with the same phrase, a proof perhaps of the rapidity with which Cæsar wrote, as much as of the unadorned nature of his style.

'**deligitur, persuadet.**' The historic present, so constantly employed by Latin historians, ought to be translated in English by the past tense. The Latin language, far more rhetorical than our own, loves to represent past events as if going on under the reader's eye; in English a past tense is more dignified.

4 '**regnum.**' Royal power had fallen into disuse in Gaul in the generation before Cæsar. It had never been hereditary, but was granted by the voice of the nation. During Cæsar's wars it was conferred for the last time by the Arvernians on Vercingetorix. See Introd. p. 30.

5 '**Dumnorix, Divitiacus.**' Dumnorix was the leader of the national or anti-Roman party among the Æduans. Divitiacus was one of the chief Druids, and therefore possessed great influence throughout all Gaul, a nation *admodum dedita religionibus;* but he was the leader of the Romanizing party. This division between the two brothers is typical of the dissension and party strife which was the ruin of Gaul.

'**qui, principatum, plebi,**' *qui* is Dumnorix; *princ.* may be rendered "ascendency," or a "preponderating influence;" it does not mean any acknowledged official power, but influence derived from birth, wealth, and energy. *Plebs* may be rendered "populace," "popular," or even "national party." Cæsar always uses words familiar to Roman ears in describing the political and social relations of the Gauls, to which the Roman terms are only applicable in a very partial degree. The Gallic *plebs* was composed of the Æduan priests and knights, while the Roman *plebs* was at this time in great measure a needy populace.

'**conaretur,**' imp. subj. after *persuadet,* a historic present.

6 '**Perfacile factu.**' This sentence should be translated in English as a quotation, in the very words used by Orgetorix. To do this *probat* should be made parenthetical. "It is a very simple thing," so he assured them, "to attain these objects, because I," &c.

'**totius Galliae**' = *civitatum totius Galliæ;* partitive genitive after *plurimum.*

7 '**potiri.**' Here with genitive; elsewhere in Cæsar it has the ablative. The genitive after *potiri* is in classic writers almost confined to the phrase *rerum potiri.*

'**posse sperant.**' *Spero* is regularly followed by a future inf., but as *possum* has no future, the present is used ; for other verbs without a future infin., the periphrase *fore ut* should be used.

CHAPTER IV.

'**ex vinclis,**' "from his imprisonment;" contrary to custom at Rome, where the accused remained free till sentence was pronounced against him, and often anticipated a condemnation by going into exile. It does not mean that he spoke in chains. 1

'**familiam, clientes.**' *familia* = personal retinue of servants and slaves. *clientes* = vassals, who followed a powerful chief from birth or friendship, or from fear and need of protection. Vassals of the noblest class were bound to live and die with their chief. 2

'**se eripuit.**' He was not set free, for he died in confinement. Cæsar only means to say that the magistrate was overawed by the multitude from pronouncing judgment.

'**rem,**' thing, *i.e.* "defiance of authority." 3

'**magistratus.**' See Introd. p. 30.

The story of Orgetorix, as related by Cæsar, is not altogether intelligible. We are told that Orgetorix, to gratify his private ambition, proposed to his countrymen to leave their lands in a body; the scheme was eagerly adopted, and scrupulous preparations were made for carrying it into effect. During these preparations a rumour arose that Orgetorix was plotting to secure royal power, and his unpopularity became so great that he laid violent hands on himself. Nevertheless, the project of migration, which was due to him, was continued as eagerly as ever.

Probably we shall be nearer the truth in considering that the desire of the Helvetians to migrate was a national feeling, not due to the ambition of Orgetorix, but to a nomadic instinct, which had once been commonly felt by Celtic tribes, and had not yet wholly passed away. Fear of German inroads may have added a spur to the feeling. Orgetorix put himself at the head of the popular movement, and became so powerful that he aimed at securing absolute power. This would irritate the nobility, who probably obtained his assassination.

CHAPTER V.

'**id quod constituerant**' = "their resolution.' 1

'**oppida**' are defensible towns, constructed on a position of natural strength, and surrounded with walls of wood and stone. 2

'**vici**' are defenceless hamlets or villages, whose inhabitants, in time of danger, fled with all their cattle and movable possessions

6 *

to the shelter of an *oppidum*. ' aedificia ' are isolated houses,
farms, &c. The number of towns and villages in a single tribe
is remarkable.

'mensum,' an older form of *mensium*. The genitive defining
the time is a somewhat peculiar use of the possessive genitive;
" belonging to," *i.e.* " required for " three months.

' molita cibaria.' The only method of grinding corn then in
use was by the cumbrous hand-mill of stone; hence stores of corn
already ground made the baggage required for the vast host
much smaller.

3 'Rauricis.' The Raurici were a Celtic tribe, who lived on the
bank of the Rhine between the Aar and Basle. The Tulingi and
Latovici were German tribes, living probably in the Black Forest
and along the upper waters of the Danube. The union of German
and Celt is remarkable, but the same alliance had taken place in
the year 108 B.C., when the Helvetians made common cause with
the Cimbrians.

' suis ' refers to the Raurici, ' cum iis ' to the Helvetians.
This is contrary to the strict rule of Latin writing, as *se, suus*
in a dependent clause should refer to the subject of the principal
verb, here *persuadent*. Cæsar very frequently uses *se* and *suus* in
reference to the subject of the dependent clause.

' Boios.' The Boians were a typical Celtic people; from an early
date they appear in history as wandering adventurers, finding their
chief pleasure in the field of battle. They formed settlements in
Italy at an early period, perhaps about 500 B.C., from which they
were driven out in B.C. 191 by Scipio Nasica, after a long and bloody
resistance. Some of them went northwards to Noricum, *i.e.* Styria,
Carinthia, and Austria, where they repelled an attack of the
Cimbrians, but had afterwards been forced to return nearer to the
Helvetians. Mommsen places the abodes, which they had last left
in Bavaria and Bohemia, and styles them "the most harassed of all
the Celtic peoples."

' Noreiam.' The modern Neumarkt in Styria, in Cæsar's time
capital of the Taurisci. The Romans remembered the name from
the defeat of the consul Carbo there in B.C. 113 by the Cimbrians.

CHAPTER VI.

1 ' quibus itineribus.' The repetition of the antecedent with the
relative gives an exactness and quaint simplicity to the style. So
below, *diem, qua die.*

'possent, ducerentur,' subjunctives after consecutive *qui* = of such a kind that.

'singuli carri,' "a single line of waggons." It has been calculated that the Helvetians must have had sixty thousand waggons, with twenty-four thousand beasts of burden, to carry their families; and two thousand five hundred waggons more with twelve thousand beasts for their baggage. The first route mentioned by Cæsar is by the right bank of the Rhone at the southeastern extremity of Mount Jura, where the river runs close beneath the steep mountain side. This spot is now named the *Pas de l'Écluse*.

'Allobrogum.' The Allobrogians were a powerful Celtic tribe 2 who lived on the left bank of the Rhine from Lake Leman to the Isère, in the modern Dauphiné and Savoy. Vienna, nineteen miles south of the present Lyons, was their capital. They had been conquered by Fabius Maximus (B.C. 121), and their lands were made a part of the Roman Province. In B.C. 61, they rose in rebellion against the extortions of Roman usurers, and in the next year, 60, *nuper*, two years before the time of which Cæsar writes, had been pacified by the prætor, C. Pomponius.

'vado transitur,' is forded, *i.e.* "is fordable," for otherwise it could not be done.

'Genava.' Geneva, at the western extremity of Lake Leman, on the left bank of the Rhone. The opposite bank was Helvetian soil.

'quod viderentur,' subjunctive because the clause forms part 3 of what the Helvetians thought. *quod Rhodanus fluit*, above, is a reason given by the narrator himself, therefore indicative.

'suos,' referring to the subject of *paterentur*, 'eos' to the principal subject. See note on *suis* c. 5. 3.

'qua die, is dies,' *dies* feminine = the appointed time; *dies* masc. 4 = the day of the month.

'a. d. V. Kal. Apr.' March 28th according to the calendar of the time, which was in great confusion, and did not correspond with the natural year. By the corrected or Julian calendar the date is April 16th according to Kraner, but von Goeler, with more probability, makes it correspond with March 24th, the spring equinox, with which the summer season, or time for military operations, was supposed to begin. See Chronology of the Campaign, p. 117. Cæsar gives the date to show the importance which he attaches to it, as if he were saying: "Open hostilities were to begin on the 28th of March."

'L. Pis. et A. Gab. cons.' Cæsar's successors in the consulship, B.C. 58.

CHAPTER VII.

1 ' id, eos iter facere conari,' "the fact that they;" the insertion of *id* gives definiteness to the style.

' ab urbe.' After resigning his consulship, Cæsar stayed for some months in the neighbourhood of Rome. See Introd. p. 15.

' quam max. pot. itiner.' Plutarch tells us that he reached Geneva in eight days. The distance is about 700 Roman miles. Suetonius says that Cæsar sometimes travelled 100 miles in a day.

' Provinciae.' Further Gaul; he ordered to the field all the defensive militia of the Province.

2 ' legio una.' This was the Tenth Legion, which acquired such glory in the ensuing campaigns, and was always devotedly attached to Cæsar's person and fortunes. The standard-bearer of the Tenth Legion was the first Roman soldier to set foot on the shore of Britain.

imperat,' with accus. and dat. = "orders to supply." Observe the rhetorical force of the omission of the copula.

3 'mittunt qui dicerent,' imperf. subj. after historic present; as in c. 3. 5. The words after *dicerent*, all that the envoys said, should be translated in the direct form. Reported words in Latin are equivalent to quotations in English writers.

4 ' L. Cassium consulem.' In the year B.C. 107, the Helvetians, stimulated by the example of the Cimbrians, formed an alliance with them, and left their homes to seek more quiet settlements in Western Gaul. " Under the leadership of Divico, the forces of the Tougeni and of the Tigurini (on the lake of Murten) crossed the Jura, and reached the territory of the Nitiobriges (about Agen on the Garonne). The Roman army under the consul L. Cassius Longinus, which they here encountered, allowed itself to be decoyed into an ambush, in which the general himself and his legate, the consular Gaius Piso, along with the greater portion of the soldiers, met their death. Gaius Popillius, the interim commander-in-chief of the force which had escaped to the camp, was allowed to withdraw under the yoke on condition of surrendering half the property which the troops carried with them, and furnishing hostages. So perilous was the state of things for the Romans, that one of the most important towns in their own province, Tolosa, rose against them, and placed the garrison in chains."—*Mommsen*, vol. 3, 182.

5 ' diem,' "a certain time." *Dies* in this sense is usually feminine.

Chapter VIII.

'**ea legione, militibusque.**' No preposition is used because 1 the legion and men are regarded as simple instruments in the hand of the general. The same thought appears in the use of the word *manus* = "a body of soldiers," *i.e.* the commander's *hand*, or instrument to do his will.

'**murum perducit.**' By these great defensive works, Cæsar at once revealed his mastery of the principles of Roman warfare. The works were raised to prevent the passage of the Rhone between Geneva and the Pas de l'Écluse, already mentioned, a distance of 19 Roman miles. They were by no means continuous, as the southern bank of the Rhone is for the most part precipitous, and naturally impassable. Only the more open points were rendered impregnable; at such points the *murus* presented to the enemy the following front, which formed the *munitiones* or line of defence.

Behind this line were *castella* or redoubts, strong forts in which the *praesidia* or detachments of soldiers, were safe from attack. Napoleon considered that he had found traces of four *castella*.

'**quo facilius.**' In oratio recta his words would be: "*eo faci-* 2 *lius, si me invito transire conabuntur, prohibere potero.*"

'**more et exemplo,**' "according to the principles and precedents 3 of the Roman government."

'**ostendit,**' "makes no secret," "assures them;" *ostendo* implies the demeanour and gesture of the speaker.

'**concursu militum.**' The soldiers in the detachments came 4 up in strength to the point attacked. B. ii. c. 33. *ex proximis castellis eo concursum est*, where a similar defence is described.

'**Helvetii—destiterunt.**' This Latin period should be rendered by breaking it up, so as to form several sentences in English. "The

Helvetians, thus disappointed, joined boats together and constructed a number of rafts; detachments also (*alii*) made repeated
attempts, sometimes by day, but more commonly during the night,
to force a passage by crossing at the fords, where the river is
shallowest; but these attempts were all beaten back by the strength
of the lines, by rallies of defenders to the points assailed, and by
showers of missiles, and at last came to an end."

Chapter IX.

1 '**una via,**' "but one route," *i.e.* the narrow passage by the Pas
de l'Écluse.

2 '**sua sponte,**' "by their own unassisted efforts."

'**impetrarent,**' "obtain their end," the object is not expressed.

3 '**gratia,**' "popularity."

Chapter X.

1 '**Cæsari renuntiatur,**' "word was brought back," *i.e.* Cæsar
had sent out spies, friendly Gauls, to inform him of the Helvetian
movements. He was always most systematic in procuring information of his enemies' intentions.

'**Æduorum.**' The Æduans were a powerful Celtic tribe, who
had long been allies of Rome. Cæsar professed to restore them to
the pre-eminence in Gaul which they had previously claimed, but
irretrievably lost in their defeat by Ariovistus. (See Introd. p. 8.)
Their lands lay in the heart of Gaul, extending from Autun, southwards to Lyons, and westwards to the Loire. Their capital was
Bibracte (*Mont Beuvray*, nine miles from Autun), and their other
chief towns, Noviodunum (*Nevers*), Cabillonum (*Châlons-sur-Saône*),
and Matisco (*Macon*).

'**Santonum.**' The Santoni (for the genitive is irregular) lived in
the west of Gaul, in the valley of the, Charente, between the
Garonne and the Loire. The modern *Saintonge* and the town
Saintes retain their name.

'**Tolosatium finibus.**' Cæsar was about to do two unconstitu-
tional things, to step beyond the limits of his Province, and to enrol
fresh legions without having first obtained the consent of the senate.
It was therefore important for him to show that he was forced to
override technical considerations by an immediate danger threatening the Province and Rome, for *salus populi, summa lex.* The
danger was real, though the Santoni were not near the Roman
border; the frontier of Toulouse was weak (*loca patentia*), and
Cassius had previously been defeated in the Garonne valley, when

the people of Toulouse had at once risen against the Roman garrison. On Cæsar's further views, see Introd. p. 15.

'**Titum Labienum.**' Labienus was the ablest of Cæsar's lieu- 3 tenant-generals. Throughout the war he always received from Cæsar the most important independent commands, and, in Cæsar's annual absences in Italy, was left in charge of the army in Gaul. It is therefore remarkable that in the Civil War he deserted Cæsar and joined Pompey, and perhaps even more remarkable that, when severed from his great chief, he showed no conspicuous military talent, save perhaps at Munda, where he fell.

'**duas legiones conscribit.**' The eleventh and twelfth legions, enrolled on Cæsar's own authority. It should be observed that the number of a legion was not a permanent title like that of a modern regiment. A legion was enrolled for a special purpose, received a number convenient at the time, and served under that name till it was disbanded, and the name ceased for the time to exist.

'**tres.**' These three legions were the seventh, eighth and ninth, which the senate had already conferred on Cæsar. These three, with the tenth, are the "veteran legions" of the Gallic War; the others, in spite of their gallant service, never acquired this name. So much training and experience of war was required to make a Roman soldier.

'**Aquileiam.**' An important military station, founded 183 B.C., to defend the N.E. of Italy against the inroads either of Illyrian or of Alpine tribes.

'**qua proximum iter.**' He marched up the valley of the Po to Turin, and then ascending the Dora Riparia he crossed the pass of the Mont Genèvre. He was now in the valley of the Durance, where he descended probably to Embrun, when he turned north-wards to the valley of the Isère, taking the left bank of the river till he reached Grenoble, where the river bends to the west. Here Cæsar would cross, and be in the friendly country of the Allobroges. He was first attacked by the Graioceli, in the valley of the Dora Riparia; next by the Caturiges (*Chorges*) near the source of the Durance; lastly by the Ceutrones, on the upper Isère.

Cæsar probably marched to Vienna, the capital of the Allobroges, and, on receiving news there of all that had happened in his pro-tracted absence, at once crossed the Rhone, and was among the Segusiavi.

'**loca superiora,**' "heights commanding the road." 4

'**itinere,**' abl. of separation after *prohibere*.

'**compluribus, pulsis.**' Two ablatives in different construc- 5 tions interlace with each other; '**complures**' = " numerous," " a considerable number."

'**Ocelo.**' The hamlet of the Graioceli in the valley of the Dora Riparia; it is probably a Celtic word = " pass."

'**extra provinciam.**' For many reasons, Cæsar was resolved to be trammelled by no constitutional checks; and the entreaties of the Æduans and Allobroges, whose lands were being harried by the invaders, gave him a welcome pretext for leaving his province, as the appeal to Roman honour was a sufficient justification.

CHAPTER XI.

1 '**jam,**' "by this time," or "during this interval," for Cæsar had been absent for some time. Aquileia is more than four hundred Roman miles distant from Vienna; the time required to levy two legions and bring them to the field, with the difficult march over the Alps, must involve an interval of nearly two months (see p. 116). But Cæsar was now in a very different position; he was at the head of six legions, for Labienus quickly joined him; the average number of men in one of his legions is reckoned by Mommsen at 3500, by other writers at 5000; his army then was about 25,000 strong.

'**angustias,**' the defile of L'Écluse. The Sequani lay between the Jura and the Saône. The fact that the Helvetians had only advanced eighty miles in the time that Cæsar had travelled eight hundred was due to the enormous number of waggons and animals which had to pass the narrow and difficult defile.

2 '**Ædui.**' The Æduans were named allies of Rome in B.C. 121, for they only saw in the Romans the conquerors of their own old rivals, the Arvernians. Afterwards they claimed a relationship by descent with the Romans, and are named *fratres et consanguinei* by Cæsar and other Latin writers. They probably did this by inventing some equally foolish and fanciful legend, connecting the Æduans with the wanderings of Æneas.

'**nostri**' = *Romani*, as often in Cæsar, who writes as a Roman to Romans; so *liberi eorum* should strictly be *sui*, but Cæsar writes as if he were himself the speaker.

3 '**Ædui Ambarri,**' sometimes simply **Ambarri**, the Æduans about the Arar, ἀμφ' Ἀραριν; they lived chiefly on the left bank of the river north of Lyons.

'**depopulatis,**' used passively here.

5 "**fortunis**" = "fortunes," possessions; *fortuna* in sing. = "the position in life" in which a man is placed by fortune.

CHAPTER XII.

'**Flumen est Arar.**' The abrupt transition is again borrowed from [1] the language of epic poetry (see note on c. 2. 1), and gives a grace of quaintness and simplicity to the style, without the use of any archaic word, which Cæsar was very careful to avoid. He said that a chief rule in writing was to "avoid an unusual word like a sunken reef," *tamquam scopulum effugere inusitatum verbum.*

'**transibant,**' imperfect, "were engaged in crossing," "had partially crossed." They were probably endeavouring to effect the passage about twelve miles to the north of Lyons. Cæsar has not stated his own movements since he was among the Segusiavi, but he is now *citra Ararim*, and to have received accounts from the Ambarri, Æduans and Allobrogians, he must have been near the site of the modern Lyons.

'**exploratores**' = "reconnoitrers," or "a reconnoitring party;" [2] *exploratores* were detachments of men under officers. The word must not be confused with *speculatores* — "spies," who went out individually.

'**de tertia vigilia,**' "from the time of the third watch," *i.e.* "during the third watch." The night (from sunset to sunrise) was divided into four watches; from six to nine, from nine to twelve, from twelve to three, and from three to six. Cæsar therefore started "after midnight."

'**impeditos**' = "struggling under their baggage and entangled in [3] the stream." The Helvetians had set no patrols, though the Roman army was so near; their conception of warfare was only simple and rude.

'**pagus,**' a "canton" or independent division of the tribe. [4]

'**L. Cassium.**' See note on c. 7. 1.

'**sive casu, sive,**' "was it accident, or the will of heaven?" [5]

'**L. Pisonis.**' Cæsar, a year before this time, had married [6] Calpurnia, daughter of the consul of the present year. Mr. Trollope writes very scornfully of Cæsar for pretending to care about his "wife's grandfather," as compared with the loss of Helvetian life. This is to judge ancient history too much by modern standards; Cæsar had avenged a national defeat, and the news of his victory would be received with joy by all Romans. It was no unnatural satisfaction that the stain on his wife's house was also in a measure effaced.

CHAPTER XIII.

1 ' pontem in Arare faciendum curat,' " had a bridge made over the Arar; " *in Arare*, because the piles were driven amid the water. Observe the gerundive with *curare* = "to have a thing done." Every Roman legion had a special corps of pioneers (*fabri*), consisting of expert carpenters, smiths, and masons, acting under able architects and engineers ; hence the rapidity with which this bridge was constructed.

2 ' intellegerent ' = " observed," " noticed."
' legatos,' " envoys ; " *legatus* is any one deputed to represent another ; hence its common meaning " lieutenant-general."
' Divico.' As this chief had commanded the army which defeated Cassius forty-nine years before, he must now have been an aged and venerable man, of at least eighty years.
' egit ' = " spoke." *i.e. causam egit*, " pleaded his cause."

3 " Si pacem," &c.—On the nature of *Oratio Obliqua*, and the proper way in which it should be translated, see Appendix at page III.

4 ' adortus esset,' " had risen upon," " surprised."
' suae virtuti, ipsos,' *ipsius virtuti* and *se* would have been more strict Latin.
' tribueret ' = " give too much weight to ; " no object is expressed.

6 ' committeret ut,' " effect that." " Beware lest it be due to you, that," &c.
' memoriam proderet,' " hand down a name to posterity." The Helvetians had been exasperated by Cæsar's refusal to allow them to cross the Rhine at Geneva, and by the loss of their friends. The tone of Divico's answer made any terms between Cæsar and his opponents impossible.

CHAPTER XIV.

1 ' His,' " to the envoys ; " had it been " to these words," it would have been *ad haec*.
' alicuius ' for *cuius* after *si* = " of any wrongdoing whatsoever."
' difficile fuisse ' = *non fuit difficile*, 'it would not have been difficult,' of orat. recta. So *longum est* = 'it would be tedious,' *satius est*, &c. *Fuisset* in orat. recta will be unaltered.

2 ' eo invito ' = *se invito*. With ' posse ' *se* is omitted ; it is

infinit. because it represents *Num possum?*, a question of the first person, of oratio recta.

'**Allobrogas.**' An accus. of Greek form, not uncommon in the names of Gallic tribes.

'**sua, se,**' both refer to the Helvetians, and not to Cæsar, the 3 speaker. '**imp. tulisse inj.**' "to carry their misdeeds unpunished," " escape punishment for their misdeeds."

'**eodem pertinere,**' "has reference to the same end," *i.e.* "leads me to the same conclusion," *viz.* to attack the Helvetians, confident that retribution is in store for them at last. The subject to *pertinere* is contained in the two preceding clauses; *quod gloriarentur* = " your boasting."

'**consuesse enim.**' This reflection, that Providence exalts men to prosperity in order to make their subsequent fall a lesson to themselves and to others, is very frequent in the Greek poets and in Herodotus, but reads somewhat strangely in the military *ultimatum* of a practical Roman general.

'**sint,**' as if a present tense had preceded. '**facturos,**' the subject 4 *eos* omitted.

'**Hoc responso**' may perhaps be rendered " with these words 5 of defiance." Divico showed his defiance in not waiting for an answer.

CHAPTER XV.

'**equitatus.**' Cæsar's cavalry, which consisted entirely of Gallic 1 auxiliaries and of no Romans except a few officers, was an untrustworthy branch of the army. Their feelings were often in favour of the enemy, hence their defeat.

'**qui videant,**' pl. relative with sing. antecedent. Yet Cæsar would not write *equitatus praemissi sunt*.

'**alieno loco,**' "ground not their own," "unfavourable ground." 2 Cæsar was always very careful not to give battle without possessing the advantage of the ground (*suus locus*). For this he had two reasons ; the moral effect of even a slight reverse to him would have been very great among the Gauls, exciting the hope of his final defeat ; next, like all good generals, he was very careful of the lives of the soldiers who fought so bravely and toiled so incessantly in his cause.

'**nonnumquam,**' "from time to time ;" placed after *consistere* to 3 avoid the awkwardness of two adverbs coming together.

'**in praesentia,**' acc. pl. neut. 4

'**millibus,**' abl. of comparison after *amplius*. The nomin. would 5 have been equally good Latin. '**quinis**,' distributive, as it refers equally to each army.

<h2 style="text-align:center">CHAPTER XVI.</h2>

1 '**publice**,' "in the name of their government," *i.e.* through Liscus, the Vergobreth.

'**flagitare**.' The historic infin. marks his repeated, pressing demands.

2 '**frigora**' = "continuous colds," *i.e.* "cold climate."

'**pabuli**.' It must now have been June, so that the absence of grass is surprising, even granting a certain change of climate since Cæsar's time.

'**frumenta**' = "corn in the field," "growing corn;" '**frumentum**' = "corn when gathered," "stores of grain."

'**iter averterant**.' The Helvetians had moved westwards and were now in the basin of the Loire.

3 '**diem ex die ducere**,' *diem* is an accus. of time; some object should be understood with *ducere*. "They put off compliance from day to day."

'**conferri, comportari**.' "It is," they said, "being sent in to us, sent out to you, has almost reached you." The omission of any copula has a strong rhetorical force.

4 '**metiri**.' On the first of every month the Roman soldier received his ration of wheat (*menstruum frumentum*). He had to grind it himself on a hand-mill.

'**Divitiaco**.' See above c. 3. 5.

'**Vergobretum**' = "the executor of judgment." See Introd. p. 30. Till the French Revolution the Mayor of Autun was named the *Verg* or *Vierg*.

'**posset**,' imperfect although both *accusat*, the principal verb, and *sublevetur*, the principal dependent verb, are historic presents; only principal verbs stand in the historic present.

<h2 style="text-align:center">CHAPTER XVII.</h2>

1 '**privatim**' — "as individuals," "though without official station."

2 '**seditiosa atque improba**,' "rebellious and ill-affectioned." *Improbus* in prose has usually a political meaning.

3 '**praestare**,' "it is better," impers. The words from *praestare* to *erepturi* contain the arguments of Dumnorix and his friends. On the reading, see Preface.

4 '**nostra consilia**.' *Nostra* even in Oratio obliqua, because = *Romanorum*.

Chapter XVIII.

'**hac oratione**' = "this language."

'**Dumnorigem.**' See note on c. 3. 5.

'**jactari,**' "to be discussed;" *jacto* = "to toss to and fro," is applied to impassioned language of any kind.

'**esse vera,**' "that his conjecture was true."

'**summa audacia,**' the descriptive abl. or abl. of quality with 2 epithet, without addition of *virum*.

'**cupidum rerum novarum,**' "eager for political changes;" *i.e.* eager to overthrow the connection between the Æduans and Rome, and to re-establish the ancient liberties of the Æduans.

'**portoria.**' The transit-dues were a source of wealth to the Æduans, because their land lay in the centre of the natural highway between the north and south of France; *i.e.* up the valley of the Seine, and down the valleys of the Saône and Rhone.

'**redempta habere,**' "had bought in."

'**largiter posse,**' "his power extended widely," a rare expression. 4

'**ex matre**' = "by the mother's side."

'**suo nomine,**' "on his own account;" the expression is borrowed 5 from book-keeping, where *nomen* is the name entered on an account, hence often = a debt.

'**si quid accidat Romanis,**' "in case of a disaster to the 6 Romans;" Latin prefers a euphemistic expression.

'**imperio Pop. Rom.,**' "under the rule of Rome," an abl. of condition.

'**proelium equestre adversum.**' There is no *et* between the 7 adjectives because they are not co-ordinate; *praelium equestre* forms one idea = cavalry-encounter. So *multae naves onerariae*, and other phrases. '**quod pr. eq. adv.**' = *quae fuga equitum*, which explains '**initium eius fugae.**'

Chapter XIX.

'**traduxisset, curasset.**' Subjunctive because they are stated 1 as *reflections* of Cæsar; "he had, as Cæsar reflected, procured a passage;" the statement is not the fact itself, but the fact as seen by Cæsar.

'**ipsis.**' Cæsar and the Æduan government.

'**principem,**' "a man of leading position." Valerius Procillus 3 was a Romanizing Gaul; his father had twenty-five years before this received the Roman citizenship from Valerius Flaccus, the governor of Gaul, and had, as was customary, adopted his gentile name.

5 **'eius offensione animi,'** "without exciting bitter feelings on his part;" *offensio animi* forms one idea, on which *eius* depends. **'de eo statuat,'** "pass sentence upon him," *i.e.* sentence of death.

CHAPTER XX.

2 **'illa,'** "the accusations." **'doloris'** = "pain."

3 **'eum locum'** — "so high a position." **'animi'** — "feeling," "affection."

4 **'dextram prendit.'** The acknowledged form of raising a suppliant whose request was granted.

'suum dolorem,' "the insult to himself."

'adhibet' = "calls in," "has present at the interview." The meaning of the word is best seen in the phrase *adhibere medicum* = to call in a physician.

'custodes,' "secret spies." Thus Dumnorix escaped for four years. He is a remarkable person, because he plainly saw through Cæsar's design of conquering Gaul, almost before he had drawn his sword. Cæsar as clearly saw his determined opposition, and only spared him now because he felt that by executing him he would lose the support of the Æduans, which alone gave him a pretext for his position beyond the province.

CHAPTER XXI.

1 **'exploratores,'** "a reconnoitring party." See note on c. 12. 2. **cognoscerent'** — "observe," "discover."

2 **'de tert. vigil.'** See note on c. 12. 2.

'legatum pro praetore.' The *legatus* was a lieutenant-general, an assistant and representative of the commander-in-chief. He was selected by the commander, commonly from the number of ex-consuls and ex-praetors, and his selection was ratified by the senate's approval. "A *legatus* commonly commanded a legion under the general, but might also possess an independent command. In the latter case he was styled *legatus pro praetore*, and when acting under orders of the commander-in-chief he might possess the same honorary rank, as Labienus does here." *Rheinhardt.* On Labienus, see note on c. 10. 3. The senate had allowed Cæsar the unusual number of ten *legati*. In this, his first campaign, he does not seem to have had more than five acting under him (c. 52). Each of them commanded a legion, while Cæsar himself, or in his absence his quæstor P. Crassus was at the head of the remaining legion.

'**sui consilii,**' genitive after *sit*.   3

'**L. Sulla**' died B.C. 78, so that Considius must have been an old 4 soldier.

'**M. Crassi.**' Crassus, in B.C. 71, had saved Rome from great fear and danger by defeating Spartacus, the brave leader of the revolted slaves, and by slaying him on the field of battle. Considius may have served under him at that time.

CHAPTER XXII.

'**Considius**' must have given Cæsar a great disappointment, as, 1 through his weakness and fear, an opportunity of inflicting a crushing defeat was lost. Cæsar, like other great generals, had to train his officers, and we do not hear of his employing Considius again.

'**equo admisso,**' "with reins loose," *i.e.* "at full gallop."

'**cognovisse a**' = "he had recognized them *from*."

'**insignia,**' not standards = *signa*, but "devices and ornaments" in their armour, especially on helmets, which were adorned with wings, horns, and similar fantastic additions.

'**subducit, instruit.**' The omission of the copula marks the 2 rapidity of Cæsar's action, and his excitement on receiving the news; for had Considius's report been true, Labienus must have perished with his two legions.

'**multo die**' — "when day was well advanced;" so *multa nocte*, late 3 at night; *multo mane*, early in the morning.

CHAPTER XXIII.

'**biduum supererat,**' see page 117.   1

'**Bibracte,**' the ancient capital of the Æduans, is to be identified with Mont Beuvray, one of the chief heights of the mountains of Morvan. The circuit of the walls and the lines of streets are still visible on the turf; the ancient roads also converge to Mont Beuvray, which is a great argument. Until the researches of Napoleon and others it was customary to identify Bibracte with Autun. It is probable that in the early Roman period the Celtic city was removed from the mountain top, an inconvenient situation, 2500 feet high, nine miles to the east, where *Augustodunum*, the modern Autun, was constructed, and rapidly became an important and beautiful city.

2 'decurio.' A *decurio* was an under officer in the cavalry; he commanded a third portion of a *turma*, a troop or squadron, probably containing thirty-three men.

3 'existimarent.' Should properly be *existimabant;* the subjunctive with *quod* denotes a circumstance as seen and conceived by some one, here by the Helvetians. It is not therefore the fact of thinking, but the *thought as conceived* which should be in the subjunctive; yet the transition to use the verb of thinking itself in the subjunctive is very natural, and frequent in Cæsar. 'intercludi posse,' *i.e.* Romanos. 'a novissimo agmine' = "in the rear," *i.e.* of our men.

CHAPTER XXIV.

1 'animum advertit,' used as a single verb with a direct accusative.

2 'triplicem aciem.' The veteran legions were the 7th, 8th, 9th, and 10th. See note on c. 10. The triple line was formed by an arrangement of the legion which gave to the army the advantage of having a reserve, and also of keeping the troops in movable bodies, which might in the dangerous moment of a battle be brought up to the point where safety was threatened. In each legion there were ten cohorts, from 350 to 500 men strong, and these cohorts were arranged in three lines, with a cohort's length of free space between each cohort and also between the lines. The depth that the soldiers stood is not quite certain; they were either ten or six men deep.

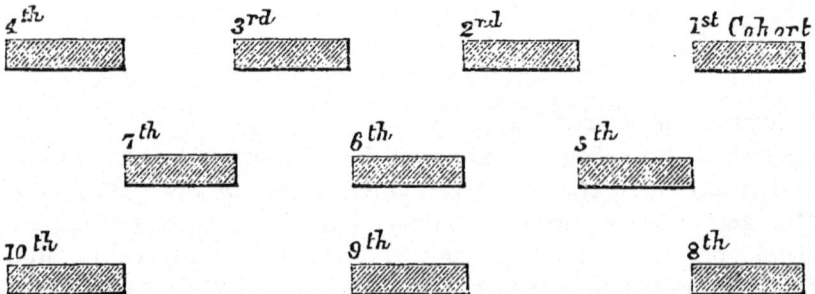

'auxilia.' The auxiliary or light-armed troops here meant were slingers from the Balearic islands who hurled stones or balls of lead (*glandes*), and Cretan archers. The slingers had only a leather jacket instead of the cuirass of the legionary, and a small round target (*parma*) instead of the heavy *scutum;* the archers had no shield. These troops were therefore not available for a close conflict; they were used for skirmishing, or when the enemy were in flight.

'**totum montem.**' The whole mountain above where he stood with the four legions.

'**sarcinas.**' *Sarcinae* was the light baggage, or the burden carried by the soldier on the march. A bundle was made up, containing provisions (*cibaria*) usually for a fortnight, cooking-vessels and an axe, and was slung over the shoulder attached to the end of a pole (*furca*). Each soldier had also to carry two stakes for the rampart (*valli*).

The *impedimenta*, or heavy baggage, consisted of tents, engines of war, supplies of arms, handmills of stone, and other necessaries; it was carried by draught animals, in the proportion of about 500 to a legion, each beast being attended by a *calo*, or camp follower.

'**carris.**' The *carrus* was a two-wheeled cart, with solid, drum- ₃ shaped wheels.

'**confertissima acie.**' Observe the repeated ablatives, marking the various features of the sudden assault.

phalange facta.' The phalanx was a dense and unbroken column, in which the shields of the foremost ranks were so interlaced as to form an advancing wall, while the mere weight of the troops pressing behind made resistance impossible.* It was the order of battle common to the Gauls and Germans of Cæsar's time, and had been employed by the Romans under the kings, and by the Greek armies of Philip and Alexander. The Roman wars with Macedon had proved that the phalanx was unwieldy, and ill-fitted to cope with the more open and manageable order of the Roman legion. The Gallic wars taught the same lesson again and again. When the Romans with their *pila* succeeded in breaking through the interlaced shields of the front line, holes were made in the dense ranks, and the mass was broken up. Once the phalanx was broken up, there was no means to make fresh dispositions, which the Romans could do by means of their legions and cohorts, at the decisive moment of a hard-fought battle. The phalanx hazarded all in the first furious charge.

---

* Homer describes the array of the phalanx and the feelings which it inspired;

οἱ δ' ἐπεὶ ἀλλήλους ἄραρον τυκτῇσι βόεσσιν,
βάν ῥ' ἰθὺς Δαναῶν λελιημένοι, οὐδ' ἔτ' ἔφαντο
σχήσεσθ', ἀλλ' ἐν νηυσὶ μελαίνῃσιν πεσέεσθαι.—Il. 12. 105.

/ *

CHAPTER XXV.

1 **'suo equo.'** Plutarch quotes Cæsar's words: "*When his horse was brought up to him, he said: 'After the victory, I shall require my horse for the pursuit; now let us fall on the enemy;' and on foot he joined in the charge.*" Cæsar's men required encouragement, for the Helvetians had a great reputation for courage in arms, and Cæsar knew how to give the encouragement required.

'omnium equis.' This does not mean the horses of the cavalry, but those of the military tribunes, of the staff, and of the young men of position serving in the army. It is very probable, from what happened shortly afterwards at Vesontio, that Cæsar had little confidence in the courage of these honorary soldiers.

2 **'pilis.'** The *pilum* was a javelin about six feet in length. The iron portion, which ended at the point, was about three feet in length, and was let into the shaft. The legionaries standing a few paces apart, each man defending his own piece of ground, swung the heavy weapon over their heads, and then hurled it down on the enemy. When the sharp, thin point pierced the enemy's shields, the weight of the shaft made the wrought iron of the point to bend.

3 **' cum,'** causal = " owing to the bending of the iron point."

'nudo corpore ' — "with their body undefended."

5 **'succedentibus '** — " ascending in pursuit."

'ex itinere' = " on the march as they were," "without further preparation."

'latere aperto' = "on the side undefended by the shield," *i.e.* " on the right flank."

6 **'conversa signa bipartito intulerunt.'** Every maniple, or body of about 120 men,—and there were three maniples in each cohort,—had a *signum*, or standard of its own. The early standards were animals, the eagle, wolf, minotaur, boar, &c.; afterwards small shields of metal with a hand at the top (pun on *manipulus*) were common devices. The standard-bearer stood at the right of the maniple, and gave the order to the line; the others took their places from him, and moved as he moved. Hence the incessant use of *signa* = the lines or ranks, more properly *ordines*. The phrases in which *signa* occurs speak for themselves; *signa conferre*, to fight with the enemy; *signa inferre*, to advance to the charge; *signa referre*, to retreat; *ad signa convenire*, to muster; *a signis discedere*, to desert; *sub signis*, in marching order; *signa convertere*, to change front, wheel.

The change of front can only have been partial; the *tertia acies*

wheeled round so as to meet the unexpected attacks. Translate ;
" by a partial change of front faced the enemy on two sides."

CHAPTER XXVI.

'ancipiti proelio,' "against a double enemy ;" *anceps* is used in 1
its strict and literal sense = two-headed, and must not be translated " a doubtful struggle."

'cum' = "although ;" fighting lasted for five hours.   2

'matarae, tragulae.' Celtic darts, of which the *tragula* was 3
the heavier. The word *matara* is retained in the modern French
matras = bolt of the crossbow.

'ad impedimenta.' Both Gauls and Germans were in the habit
of arranging their baggage-waggons in a circle, which served them
instead of a regular defensive camp. As has been seen, the number
of Helvetian waggons must have been extraordinary. Plutarch
says that both the women and children of the Helvetians fought in
defence of the baggage-train, and were cut down along with the men
by the Roman soldiers. The carnage, by Cæsar's own figures, was
enormous.

The probable locality of this great battle is much disputed, but
there is no reason to deviate from the common view, which is that of
Napoleon. Both armies were in the Loire-valley, the Helvetians in
front and Cæsar behind, when Cæsar gave up the pursuit, and took
the road for Bibracte (*Mont Beuvray*). Cæsar began to march
eastwards to Bibracte ; the Helvetians turned and offered battle in
which they faced to the east, the Romans to the west ; during the
battle the Boians came in *from the north*, as the Helvetians had been
in advance of the Romans, and so attacked the Romans on their
right flank. The actual site of the battle is supposed to have been
between Luzy and Chides, in the valley of La Roche, a small
rivulet which flows southward from Mont Beuvray, joining the
Alène, whose waters finally reach the Loire near Decize.

'Lingonum.' The Lingones lived in the Vosges mountains, 5
at the sources of the Marne and the Meuse. Their capital was
Andematunnum, the modern *Langres*, an important military station
in modern as well as in ancient times.

'die quarto,' " on the third day after the battle," as the Romans
included the day of battle itself in reckoning. The distance
traversed was about one hundred miles.

'triduum morati.' This proves the fierceness of the struggle
the Roman army was so severely handled that they required three
days to recruit, and certain critics blame Cæsar for " bolstering up "

what was nearly a defeat into a signal victory. This is not just;
Cæsar acknowledges, in his impersonal manner, the courage of the
enemy, who never showed their backs, and the wounds of his own
men. A victory is not merely decided by the events of the field of
battle, but by the consequences: however close the struggle, the
result was that Cæsar had achieved a signal and decisive victory.

6 '**nuntios ne juvarent,**' "messengers ordering them not to."
Observe *Lingonas*, a Greek form of the accus. pl. It is not
uncommon in names of Gallic tribes : see c. 14. 2. *Allobrogas.*

'**loco**' commonly, like *numero*, used without the prepos. *in.*

CHAPTER XXVII.

1 '**Qui paruerunt.**' This sentence, if rendered word for word in
English, would be awkward and harsh, and would lose the grace of
the Latin period, which lies in the rhetorical effect of the word
paruerunt. The sentence should be broken up, and might run :
"Their envoys met him on the march, threw themselves down at
his feet, and with tears and humble petitions sued for peace ; on
receiving Cæsar's command that their friends should await his
arrival on the spot where they were, they obeyed."

3 '**conquiruntur,**' *i.e. obsides et servi;* '**conferuntur,**' *i.e. arma.*

'**Verbigenus.**' This canton is said to have extended from Soleure
to Lucerne.

'**dediticiorum,**' "of prisoners," of surrendered persons ; the
termin. -*icius* added to a perfect partic. denotes the *quality* derived
from the past *act.—Roby.*

'**quod existimarent.**' See note on c. 23. 3.

CHAPTER XXVIII.

1 '**resciit**' — "ascertained from his scouts;" *re* as in *renuntio*, "to
send word back." See note on c. 10. 1.

'**sibi**' = "in his eyes." '**in hostium numero habuit**' = "he put
them to the sword ;" a euphemism.

3 '**Germani.**' Cæsar expresses his fear of a German occupation of
Switzerland ; it is probable that German aggression was an important
factor in the reasons which induced the Helvetians to seek for new
settlements.

'**Galliae prov. Allobrogibusque,**' "the Gallic province, that
is, the Allobrogians." Cæsar has already said (c. 6. 2, 10. 5) that
the Allobrogians belonged to the Province.

4 '**Boios.**' The remnant of the Boians was settled by the Æduans
on the strip of land between the Loire and the Allier near the junction

of the two rivers. They were intended to hold the border-land against the Arvernians. The statement that they were afterwards admitted to equal rights and liberties with the Æduans proves that this book was certainly revised and probably written after the seventh year of the war; for in the beginning of the seventh year they are called *stipendiarii Æduorum.* Their privileges were probably given them on account of services rendered in that year.

CHAPTER XXIX.

'Graecis litteris.' Greek letters, but in the Gallic language. 1 The Gauls, having no written characters of their own, borrowed Greek letters from the people of Massilia, as they also borrowed the art of coinage and the designs on their coins. In a similar way in earlier times the Romans had borrowed Greek letters from Cumae, which the Greeks themselves had borrowed from Phœnicia.

'ratio confecta erat, qui numerus,' = "An account had been made up detailing the number of those who."

'summa erat,' but below **'summa fuerunt.'** The number of 2 the verb is decided by the nearness of the predicate.

'rerum' here applies even to persons.

'ad milia' = "about 368,000;" *i.e.* one fighting man in every four of the population. The other numbers are accurate: this is a calculation.

'milium c et x.' 222,000 had perished in the expedition; a 3 fearful 'bloodbath.'

CHAPTER XXX.

'Galliae,' "Celtic Gaul" only, as it is throughout this chapter 1 and the next.

'Helvetiorum injuriis Populi Romani,' "wrongs done by the Helvetians to the Roman People." The first gen. is of the author or subject, the second is of the object on whom the wrongs were done.

'ex magna copia,' "from full abundance of places to choose from," *i.e.* "at their own discretion."

'stipendiarios' — "tributary;" *stipendium* was a tribute paid in money.

'concilium totius Galliæ,' "an assembly of the chiefs of all 2 Celtic Gaul." Such assemblies are frequently mentioned; their primary object was defence against some common danger, though they were abused to further the objects of ambitious leaders. To calm Cæsar's suspicion that the assembly might be directed against himself, his permission is asked before the meeting is held.

3 **'enuntiaret,'** "should publish the decisions of the assembly," the object of the verb being omitted.

CHAPTER XXXI.

1 **'salute'** = "welfare" or "interests;" *salus* is a word of wider import than the Eng. "safety."

2 **'projecerunt.'** The aged Celtic chiefs, in ornaments of gold and armour adorned with gold, with their tears and gestures, and long silvery hair flowing over their shoulders, as was the manner of suppliants, must have formed a picturesque scene, and have found a strong contrast in the grave attitude of the Roman Proconsul.

3 **'Divitiacus'** is the natural spokesman of the Romanizing Gauls. **'factiones duas.'** On the rivalry of the Æduans and Arvernians, see Introd. p. 28.

'potentatus' = "leading position," *i.e. principatus totius Galliae.*

'Germani.' On the position of the Germans in Gaul, see Introd. p. 33.

4 **'clientes'** = "their followers," *i.e.* the smaller states who formed their *factio.*

'omnem nobilitatem.' An exaggerated statement, as the nobility and the knights of the Æduans are numerous and powerful during the campaigns of Cæsar.

5 **'hospitio.'** *Hospitium publicum* was a legal relation between an independent state and Rome, and was created by the senate passing a resolution that the representatives of the state in question should receive an honourable reception in Rome, lodgings defrayed from the public exchequer, and gifts of hospitality. Divitiacus had received these attentions in Rome a few years previously. *Amicitia* was a more intimate relation, also conferred by the senate.

6 **'adduci non potuerit.'** It is possible that Divitiacus' position as one of the chief Druids may have made his person inviolable, and so given him an isolated liberty of action.

7 **'Ariovistus.'** How dramatic is this first mention of the dreaded German chief. Instead of discussing the state of Gaul and analysing all the dangers he had to meet, Cæsar allows the events to tell their own tale, and the actors to introduce themselves to the reader like the personages in a drama, with all the freshness of the surroundings in which they moved. How much better do we apprehend the danger to Gaul from Ariovistus, when we see him and his army thus

depicted to us in the words of an excited and terrified enemy, who had already suffered from his aggressions, than we should have done had Cæsar confined himself to mere narrative and disquisition. On Ariovistus and the Suebi, see Introd. p. 7.

'Harudum.' The Harudes came with the Cimbrians from the North of Jutland, and had settled between the Rhine, the Maine, and the Danube.

'sedes' = "settlements," "permanent habitation."

'neque enim conferendum,' " there was no comparison between 8 Gallic and German land ; " we should transpose the order and say, " between German and Gallic land," putting the best last.

'hanc' = Galliae, that of the speaker.

Admagetobrigae.' The battle was fought in the year 72 B.C., 9 but the locality is uncertain.

superbe et crud. imperare' — "is an arrogant and cruel tyrant."

'exempla cruciatusque' — " practises every species of torture." exemplum is an instance or single act, which may be used as a principle o serve as a warning.

'Hominem.' Observe the depreciative force of homo, increased 10 by its prominent position in the sentence.

'non posse,' sc. se; so below, se non dubitare.

'sit auxilii.' From here to the end the tenses change to the 11 present ; insensibly the speaker and the scene have been brought actually into the presence of the reader.

CHAPTER XXXII.

'earum rerum' instead of eorum quae ; Cæsar's definite style loves 1 the use of res.

'horrerent' = "shuddered at the thought of," with accus.

'tamen' = "at least," "if the worst came to the worst."

CHAPTER XXXIII.

'beneficio.' In the previous year, B.C. 59, Ariovistus had been 1 honoured with the title of king and friend by a resolution of the Roman senate. Cæsar, the presiding consul, had proposed the resolution, an act which is difficult to reconcile with the attitude which he now assumes. The explanation may perhaps be that Cæsar despaired of exciting public feeling in Rome as to the danger of German aggression, and wished to give no hint as to his own future policy in Gaul. Neither Cæsar nor Rome was committed in any way ; it was friendly to send gifts to Ariovistus, and to style him *King of the Suebi*, but no more.

2 **'secundum ea,'** "following upon these facts," *i.e.* "besides," "in addition to."

'cogitandam et suscipiendam,' "why the subject in his judgment (*putaret*) called not only for reflection, but for active interference."

'fratr. cons.' See note on c. 11. 2.

'in tanto imperio,' "considering the undisputed empire;" *tantus* should often be translated by an English adjective ; Latin, being very rhetorical in structure, uses a demonstrative pronoun to fix the attention. **'turpissimum'** = "disgraceful," "a disgrace;" English, less rhetorical than Latin, is satisfied with the positive adjective.

3 **'Cimbri Teutonique.'** On the Cimbrians and Teutons, see Introd. p. 5.

'Rhodanus,' "nothing but the Rhone," "the Rhone and no more;" a river fordable at certain points, c. 6. 2.

4 **'spiritus'** = "arrogance," "pride;" usu. in acc. pl. and in a bad sense ; in the gen. case the singular is used and more often than the pl. in a good sense ; *angebant ingentis spiritus virum Sicilia Sardiniaque amissæ.*—*Livy*, 21. 1. of Hamilcar.

This chapter is intended to show why Cæsar a second time entered upon a campaign without consent of the senate. He wishes his Roman readers to understand that they had to choose between instant war and a second Cimbrian invasion.

Chapter XXXIV.

1 **'legatos.'** Ariovistus, who could not 'sit still when kings were arming,' was probably during the Helvetian war preparing his own forces on his own frontier, *i.e.* among the Triboces, near the modern Strasburg. The distance between Langres, near where Cæsar was, and Strasburg is about two-hundred Roman miles, so that the passage of envoys to and fro must have occupied considerable time.

'medium utriusque,' "midway between both," belonging equally to both ; hence the genitive after *medius*, used as an adj. of possession. It is different from the partitive gen. usual with *medius ; regio Italiae media*, "a district in the heart of Italy."— *Livy*, 5. 54.

'si quid se velit,' "if he required him for anything;" double 2
acc., a personal object and neuter pronoun.

'possideret' = "occupied;" *possessio* properly and very com- 3
monly means only "landed possessions," on which the owner 'sits
down' (πρός, *sedeo*).

'commeatu et molimento' = "without providing large stores
and putting forth great exertions."

'esset.' The reader will not fail to observe in this chapter the
rude and abrupt manner of the proud German chief, and the direct-
ness of his replies. Cæsar has not the advantage in argument, but
when conqueror meets conqueror, the better sword is the better
argument.

CHAPTER XXXV

'mandatis' = "demands," "ultimatum;" Cæsar would not parley 1
further.

'permitteret ut liceret,' a *very* polite pleonasm. 2

'fecisset, impetraret,' in oratio recta, *fecerit* and *impetrabit.* 3

'M. Messalla, L. Pisone,' B.C. 61, three years before.

'censuisset, uti.' *censeo ut* = "I give my opinion to the effect
that;" *censeo rem ita esse* — "I state my opinion that the fact
is so."

'quod' "in so far as;" the simple relative in its restrictive
sense with the subjunctive, as in the common phrase *quod sciam* =
"so far as I know." This is better than to take *quod* as a legal
archaism and contracted for *quoad.*

commodo,' "in the interest of;" abl. of condition.

'neglecturum.' Cæsar assumes the attitude of a constitutional
proconsul, only carrying out the will of the senate.

CHAPTER XXXVI.

'Ad haec' = "to these arguments;" his = "to these persons." See 1
c. 14. 1.

'qui vicissent' = "the conquerors;" 'iis quos vicissent' =
"the conquered."

'suum arbitrium, suo jure.' *suus* refers to Populus Romanus,
though this is irregular; below *suo adventu* and *sibi* are in one clause,
suo referring to Cæsar, and *sibi* to Ariovistus. See note on c. 5. 2.

'in eo quod convenisset' = "the stipulated terms," "the agree- 4
ment." *convenit* = "it is agreed."

'iis,' dat. after *afuturum; abesse* here used in the sense of *deesse* =
"fail to help them."

5 'quod denuntiaret' "as to the circumstance that you threaten me," as to your threats." Before *neminem*, "I have no fears," or some such clause should be supplied; Ariovistus speaks very briefly, and does not give full expression to his thought.

'intellecturum' — "you will find out;" *intelligo* usu. = to observe, notice, rather than to "understand."

'annos xiv.' These words give the date of the entrance of the Germans into Gaul, 72 B.C.

'tectum non subiissent,' "had not come beneath a roof." The expression is undoubtedly exaggerated; the meaning is that all this time they had had no settled habitation.

CHAPTER XXXVII.

1 'Treveris.' The Trevirs were a tribe of Celtic Gaul, who lived on the course of the Moselle. They boasted themselves of German descent, and their cavalry was famous. Their names remains in the modern Tréves, on the Moselle, which was their capital.

'fines eorum,' for *suos;* yet in the next clause *sese* is used.

'pacem Ariov.' "friendly treatment from Ariovistus."

2 'pagos centum Sueborum.' The so-called Suebian tribe (probably, as a residential tribe, to be identified with the Chatti), contained a hundred divisions or cantons, each of which annually sent a thousand men to the field. The news therefore is of a second German invasion; not a mere reinforcement of Ariovistus, but a new invasion of the whole Suebian soldiery. They were on the Rhine about Mayence, which is opposite the country of the Trevirs. Cæsar might well be alarmed, for had they formed a junction with Ariovistus, 200,000 Germans might have proved too much for his six legions.

'ad ripas' = "on the bank," *i.e.* at different places on the right bank; it does not mean "on both banks."

CHAPTER XXXVIII.

1 'Vesontio' (masc.) is the modern Besançon, on the Doubs, which is now, just as Vesontio was in Cæsar's time, the most important frontier fortress in France towards the Upper Rhine, which, at the passage of Belfort, contains the natural entrance from Germany into France.

'quod.' The relative is commonly attracted, as here, into the gender of a substantive standing as predicate in the relative clause.

2 'facultas' = "abundance."

'ad ducendum bellum' = "to protract the war."

3 'pedum mille sexcentorum.' The MS. have only *sexcentorum,*

but as the actual measurement of the neck is now 1620 Roman feet, it is probable that *mille* has been lost. See Preface.

'**magnis nocturnis itiner.**' On the double adj. see note on 4 c. 18. 7. *Nocturnis* is put before *diurnis* with emphasis, as if to say, "by night as well as by day." An ordinary march, *justum iter*, was performed in six or seven hours, and consisted of twenty Roman miles; a forced march in eight or nine hours, with a corresponding increase in distance.

'**occupato oppido.**' By his promptitude in seizing Vesontio, Cæsar had obtained four great advantages, (1) supplies for the moment, (2) a strong base of operations, (3) control over the war, for his enemy could not now escape him, and (4) power to confine the war to the Rhine-valley.

CHAPTER XXXIX.

'**Dum—moratur.**' The panic and mutinous feeling which spread among the legions at Vesontio are often ascribed to the evil effect of the delay and inactivity of these few days; not quite justly, for though the delay was the occasion of the mutiny, more general reasons must be found for the cause. It is the first and only mutiny of Cæsar's soldiers throughout the long and laborious Gallic campaigns; it also arose immediately after a great victory, arguments that it arose from peculiar causes. Perhaps, if we realize the position of the army, it was not unnatural. They had penetrated the central districts of Gaul, hitherto independent and unknown, and had with difficulty overcome a nation confessedly inferior to the Germans in military courage and skill. Wearied by a week of forced marches, they looked out from the height of Vesontio on the towering Jura, on the dark valley of the Doubs, and on the impenetrable forests beyond which their enemy lay. Their general was not an old soldier, and seemed possessed by an imperturbable foolhardiness; moreover the senate had not authorized the war, not even the first departure from the province. When opinions of this kind were expressed by the officers of the army, they naturally spread through the rank and file. Cæsar depicts the dismay of these 'delicate soldiers' with a humour which he rarely allows to his unimpassioned pen.

'**commeatus,**' "other necessaries;" a more general word than *res frumentaria.*

'**percontatione**'="the minute inquiries;" the word suggests the fear of the inquirer.

'**vocibus**' = "conversation," "replies."

'**congressos**,' "had met them in battle;" the Gauls only said this.

'**non mediocriter**,' a litŏtes = "in an extraordinary degree."

'**mentes animosque**.' *Mens* = "power of thought;" *animus* = feeling, will, "power of action." The distinction is very important, and is well illustrated by the two following quotations: Cæsar B. G. iii. c. 19, says, *Nam ut ad bella suscipienda Gallorum alacer ac promptus est* animus, *sic mollis ac minime resistens ad calamitates perferendas* mens *eorum est*, where *animus*, the enthusiastic spirit or temper, which shows itself in immediate action, is contrasted with *mens*, deep-set resolution, based not on impulse and feeling, but on a matured and unaltered purpose.

Livy (37, 45) thus, in the mouth of Scipio, describes the temper of Roman government. *Romani ex iis quae in deum immortalium potestate erant, ea habemus, quae dii dederunt;* animos, *qui nostrae* mentis *sunt, eosdem in omni fortuna gessimus gerimusque; neque eos secundae res extulerunt, nec adversae minuerunt.* "Of those material gifts, which it lay at the discretion of Providence to bestow, we Romans possess the share which Providence has given us; but our temper depends upon our own judgment; and through every change in outward position we have preserved and still preserve the same temper, in prosperity not elated, and in adversity not dismayed."

2 '**ortus est a**' = "began with."

'**tribuni militum**.' Each legion was ordinarily under the command of a *legatus*, but in addition six *tribuni militum* were attached, each of whom was on duty for two months of the year, and, subject to the legatus, was in command of the legion. All the *tribuni militum* were men of rank, who had never served as common soldiers; they had been in the *cohors praetoria* for two years, and were usually selected out of this body by the commander-in-chief to hold the rank of tribune. Throughout all the Gallic wars only one *tribunus militum* was a distinguished officer, Volusenus, and his name is not stainless; another, it should be said, Laberius Drusus, died bravely on the field of battle.

'**praefectis**.' The *praefecti* were officers appointed by the commander-in-chief over the non-legionary troops; over auxiliaries, cavalry, *evocati* or any special body of troops. They, as well as the *tribuni*, belonged to the knightly order.

'**amicitiae causa**' = "political intimacy," perhaps, rather than "private friendship." Cæsar, like other party leaders, found appointments for the youthful relations of his partizans, which they would not have received from their merit alone.

' remanebant ' — " were ready to remain behind."

' vultum fingere ' = " to put restraint upon their looks," " to hide 3 their feelings."

' Volgo.' " Everywhere throughout the camp there was signing and sealing of wills." Evidently these officers *non magnum in re militari usum habebant.*

' quique,' " and officers who." 4

CHAPTER XL.

' consilio ' = " a council of war ; " though not in the ordinary 1 sense, because Cæsar did not summon his officers to ask their advice, but to give his own. To an ordinary council of war the *centuriones primorum ordinum*, the ten senior centurions of each legion, were summoned, but not the junior centurions. This council consisted of five legates, thirty-six military tribunes, and three hundred and sixty centurions ; Cæsar wished to imbue *every officer in the army* with his own unyielding spirit.

' vehementer eos incusavit ' = " he reproached them bitterly."

' judicaret ' = *judicet*, deliberative subjunctive, of oratio recta. 2

' vererentur ' = *veremini* of orat. recta, a question of the second 4 person.

' diligentia ' = " fidelity to my duties ; " thoughtfulness and minute discharge of all that was required ; it is the peculiar duty of a commander-in-chief. So St. Paul says : " He that ruleth, with diligence." The opposite quality is *temeritas*, thoughtlessness, recklessness.

' Cimbris et Teutonis.' See Introd. p. 5. 5

' cum videbatur.' A remarkable transition from indirect to direct language.

' servili tumultu.' The slave war lasted from 73 to 71 B.C. The slaves consisted for the most part of Germans taken prisoner by Marius, and Spartacus, the leader, was said to be the son of a German chief.

' quos,' *i.e. servos*, understood in *servili*.

' quae,' neuter, referring to *usus ac disciplina*, " things which they had learnt from us." With abstract substantives this is, perhaps, the general rule ; Livy writes, " *ira et avaritia imperio potentiora erant.*" " Rage and greed were more powerful *things* than the general's commands."

' inermos ' = " half-armed," rarer form for *inermes*. The slaves 6 had risen from the estates which they were forced to keep, using wattles covered with sheepskin as shields, and with pickaxes roughly worked into swords and spears.

8 '**sui potestatem fecisset,**' "had offered battle."

'**ratione et consilio**' = "by wise forethought." See note on c. 1. 3. *ratio* = system, calculation ; *consilium* = wisdom.

9 '**capi**' = *decipi* = "to be taken in," "caught," "duped."

11 '**frumentum, frumenta.**' See note on c. 16. 2.

'**Leucos.**' The Leuci lived in the upper valleys of the Moselle and Meuse.

12 '**avaritia**' = "peculation," embezzlement of public money; '**innocentia**' = "the purity of my hands."

13 '**repraesentaturum,**' "I will do sooner than I had intended ;' litt. "to put back into the present;" the word commonly means to "pay in ready money."

'**pudor atque officium**' = "honour and duty."

'**de quarta vigilia.**' See note on c. 12. 2.

14 '**decima legione.**' By this mark of his confidence Cæsar not only gained for ever the devotion of the Tenth Legion, but also created in the other legions a spirit of honourable rivalry to prove themselves as brave as the Tenth. The whole speech deserves a close attention ; the chief feeling which it inspires in the reader is a sense of the strong personality of Cæsar; his calmness and judgment appear more clearly in the light of the universal panic, which they are able to counterbalance, and to change into military enthusiasm. The arguments employed are natural and just : first is an argument based upon military and professional duty ; next are appeals to reason and judgment, to show that the enemy is not to be feared, and that heir general deserves their confidence. Lastly, when all arguments are satisfied, is an appeal to military duty and personal honour, the dearest feelings of a soldier. The speech illustrates well Cæsar's description of his own oratory : it is στρατιωτικοῦ λόγος ἀνδρός, "the blunt speech of a soldier." In speaking he used excessive action and gesticulation, a great contrast to his written style. The speech has also this claim on our interest, that is the best example extant of the oratory of Cæsar, so great a power in his own time.

'**praetoriam cohortem**' = "body-guard."

CHAPTER XLI.

1 '**mentes**' = "the thoughts of all;" Cæsar claims to have nfluenced their better judgment, and not merely their feeling.

'egerunt, satisfacerent' = "had discussions with,' *i.e.*, 2 "entreated their tribunes and leading centurions to make their apologies to Cæsar." Before *se* supply in English : "they said " or " saying ;" the Latin infin. shows of itself that it is a quotation, the words used by the soldiers.

'ex aliis' = "from among the rest"; *alii = ceteri*, here. 'ut' = 3 " so that."

'apertis locis.' Cæsar avoided the forests and passes which lay between Vesontio and Ariovistus ; in other words, he avoided the Doubs valley by turning to the left to Vesoul in the Saone valley, and thence passed through Belfort into the Rhine valley.

'profectus est.' Cæsar started at once, being anxious, now that his army was in better trim, to keep it so by giving it full employment, and no more idle time for ' making wills.'

'septimo die.' Seven days of continuous marching would 4 represent an advance of about 140 Roman miles. This would bring Cæsar's army as far down the Rhine as Kolmar. This was a very bold, even a very dangerous march. Cæsar was far from his supplies at Besançon, and the season was advanced. The Vosges mountains were on one side and the Rhine on the other, so that had he met with a reverse, escape would have been impossible.

exploratoribus.' See note on c. 12. 1.

CHAPTER XLII.

'sanitatem,' "a right judgment"; *i.e.*, to a harmony with Cæsar's 2 own views. Cæsar always regards his opponents—from an extrem Roman point of view, as if there was simply nothing to be said for their conduct. He names the Gallic patriots, who maintained to the last the independence of their country, *latrones*, and *perditi homines ;* their state of mind he calls *insania*.

'pertinacia' — "obstinacy "; it is opp. to *perseverantia* "persistence in a good cause."

'tolli' = "done away with," "prevented." 4

'Gallorum equitatui.' The previous campaign (see note on c. 15. 1.) and the intrigues of Dumnorix, had shown how untrustworthy the Gallic cavalry were ; the request of Ariovistus might naturally create the suspicion that in suggesting the appearance on horseback with mounted followers, he had an understanding with the Gallic cavalry.

'omnibus equis Gallis eq. detractis.' Cæsar had 4000 Gallic horse (c. 15) ; by taking all their horses he was able to mount the legion. The legion, therefore, was not more than 4000 men strong.

'**eo**' = "upon the horses."

5 '**non irridicule**' — "very wittily," a litotes. Nowhere else
throughout the Gallic war does Cæsar quote the words of a common
soldier : he often quotes the words and deeds of his centurions.

'**ad equum rescribere**'="is giving us a step—up or down—
into the knights." The *double meaning* cannot be rendered in English
without a periphrasis such as that suggested. To be raised to the
order of knights, whose property qualification was 400,000 sesterces,
was a rise in the social scale to the common soldier labouring for a
denarius a day; but for a soldier of the tenth legion to be classed
with the treacherous and timid Gallic cavalry was a disgrace.

Chapter XLIII.

1 '**tumulus terrenus.**' This "earthen mound of considerable
size" was probably a barrow raised in prehistoric times to perpetuate
the memory of some departed chief. It was, therefore, a fitting
rendezvous for the champions of Germany and Rome. Such cairns
are popularly termed in Germany "*Hunnengraeber*," "sepulchres of
the Huns," though their antiquity is far greater than the invasion of
Attila; many have in recent times been excavated in the valley of the
Rhine.

2 '**ex equis**' = "from horseback"; the pl. used because they were
two; so *a puero* of one person, but *a pueris* of more than one.

3 '**munera.**' Livy (30. 15) mentions gifts sent to Masinissa along
with the title of king; they were "a crown of gold, and a *patera* of gold,
a curule chair, a staff of ivory, an embroidered robe, and a tunic
worked with palm-branches."

'**hominum officiis**' = "personal services." '**aditus neque
causa**' = "claim or justification."

5 '**consuetudo**' = "habit," *i.e.*, "consistent principle." '**posset.**'
See note on *judicaret*, c. 40. 2.

6 '**in mandatis**' — "in the nature of commands," "as final
demands"; it does not mean "among his demands."

Chapter XLIV.

1 '**virtutibus**' = "mighty deeds," "exploits."

3 '**paratum decertare.**' *Paratus*, though used as an adj., is regularly
followed by an infin.

4 '**id**' = "the privilege," not simply referring to *amicitiam*, but to all
implied by the word.

'**bellum non intulerit, sed defenderit**' — "in the war I did 5 not act as an aggressor, but on the defensive."

'**hanc Galliam**' = "this portion of Gaul," *i.e.* "the north of 7 Gaul"; '**illam**' = "the south."

'**nostros fines, nos**' = *Romanorum, Romanos;* because Cæsar a Roman writes to Roman readers.

'**bello Allobrogum.**' See note on c. vi. 2. 8

'**multis se nobilibus.**' Doubtless Ariovistus spoke truly. Even 10 in Rome political feeling was so lawless that Clodius on one side, and Milo on the other, were leaders of hired bands of murderers. When Cæsar was about to start for the wilds of Gaul, his opponents must have thought that they had a great chance of getting rid of him, perhaps in battle, but, if not, otherwise.

'**discessisset, tradidisset,**' = *discesseris, tradideris* in orat. recta. 11

'**confecturum.**' The short sentences, and the excessive bluntness of tone throughout this speech again mark the character of Ariovistus, *homo barbarus et iracundus.*

CHAPTER XLV.

'**Arvernos et Rutenos.**' B.C. 121. See Introd. p. 4. The Ruteni 2 were a tribe in Southern Gaul, partly in the Province, and partly south of the Arverni, with whom they were closely connected.

antiquissimum quodque tempus' — "if precedence should 3 belong to the prior claim."

'**victam,**' "though conquered."

CHAPTER XLVI.

'**per fidem,**" "to which they had come trusting to his word." 3

'**interdixisset.**' Observe the cases after this verb; dative of 4 person, and abl. of separation.

CHAPTER XLVII.

'**ex suis legatum,**' "a member of his staff commissioned to treat." 1 *legatus* is a simple participle, and not = "a lieutenant-general." See Preface on the text.

'**Valerium Procillum.**' See note on c. 19. 3. Valerius Flaccus 3 had been governor of the Province in B.C. 83, twenty-five years before this time.

'**civitate donatus erat.**' Roman citizenship was highly prized

8 *

by the wealthy provincial, because it conferred a great social distinction, as well as the full privileges of Roman law. The benefits
involved were; (1) right of appeal, implying immunity from summary
punishment by a provincial governor; (2) a complete status of
equality in commercial contracts; (3) the right to hold civil or
military appointments under the government; (4) for the wealthy
provincial, like Cornelius Balbus of Gades, who went to Rome, the
right to a public career.

'**qua multa utebatur,**' "which Ar. frequently employed." The
Latin adj. of time not unfrequently takes the place of an English
adverb.

'**longinqua**' = *diutina*, "long-continued."

4 '**Conantis dicere.**' Ar. refused to treat them as envoys; he
would not allow them to open their lips, but insisted on regarding
them as spies. Very likely he considered that as they were not
Romans they could not be duly commissioned.

CHAPTER XLVIII.

1 '**eo consilio.**' The object of Ar. was to cut off Cæsar's com-
munications, and remain on the defensive, waiting till Cæsar, forced
to retire, as he must soon do owing to the advanced season, should
give him a favourable opportunity for striking a blow. In military
tactics the German '*barbarians*' had more real ability than the
more cultivated Celts.

2 '**ut**' = "so that."

3 '**genus hoc.**' Cæsar evidently admired the peculiar manœuvres
of the German cavalry, the more so perhaps as his own cavalry was
so weak. The reason of his admiration is the same as he gives
in describing the fighting from the war-chariots of the Britons:
"*They prove in battle as rapid as cavalry, and as stable as infantry*"
(B. iv. c. 33). At a later period he owed his own success in the final
struggle with the Gauls to the assistance which he received from a
body of German cavalry, who, on two decisive days, turned the tide
of battle against the Gauls. After the Gallic War, he also employed
German cavalry in the Civil War.

4 '**Cum his in proeliis.**' "These soldiers fought together, and in
battle the footmen served as a covering base to the horsemen; when
danger threatened their friends, they would press forward to their
support; when one was severely wounded and unhorsed, they would
form around him; when a long advance, or a rapid retreat was
necessary, practice had made them so perfect, that with but one

hand on the mane they kept up with the galloping horse." *Si quid erat durius*, a euphemism, Latin prefers not to mention the word of disaster. **'Concurrebant.'** See c. 8, *concursu*.

CHAPTER XLIX.

'**eum locum, quo in loco.**' See note on c. 6. 1.   1
'**passus sexcentos.**' Cæsar wished to force a battle, therefore he came very near the Germans, whose warlike temper was not likely to brook the immediate presence of an enemy without fighting. Cæsar's second camp hampered the position of Ariovistus very much, who had now the Vosges in his rear, and a Roman camp both on the left and on the right of his own. The advantage of the Roman legion, which could be separated or united at pleasure (*facilis partienti, facilis jungenti* Livy, 9. 19.) is apparent in the manœuvres, and also the strength of a Roman camp, as Cæsar does not fear to allow 10,000 men in their fortifications to stand the assault of the whole German forces.
'**acie triplici instructa.**' See note on c. 24. 2. In the immediate presence of the enemy, when an attack was possible at any moment, Cæsar marched in order of battle.
'**expedita**' — " in order of battle "; impeded by nothing except 3 their arms.

CHAPTER L.

'**instituto suo**'="according to his habit," "as he had pre- 1 viously done," '**pugnandi pot. fecit**' — " offered battle."
'**Tum demum.**' The temptation to fight was, as Cæsar had 2 desired, too great for the German chief to resist. The fighting, Cæsar allows, was hot; Dion Cassius asserts that Ariovistus was within an ace of storming the lesser camp.
'**proelio decertaret**' = "join in a general engagement"; the 3 attack on the lesser camp was only a partial engagement.
'**matresfamiliae.**' The Germans venerated all women and worshipped some. " They believe them to be possessed by a sacred and prophetic power, and neither fail to ask their advice, nor scorn to accept it. In the days of Vespasian Veleda was an instance, who for a long time and by many tribes was considered a deity." *Tac. Germ.* c. 9. Women with prophetic gifts were named *Alrunas*, " all-knowing."
'**sortibus**' = "by lots." " They have but one manner of taking the lot. A bough is cut off a fruit-tree; the twigs are then severed from the bough, and, after each has received a separate mark, are

thrown at hazard on a white cloth.　Then the priest of a tribe, if the tribe is asking for the oracle, or the head of the household, if the request is of a private nature, comes forward, and after prayer to the gods, with his eyes fixed on the heavens, lifts up three twigs one after the other, divining their meaning as he lifts them up from the mark previously made."　*Tac. Germ.* c. 10.

'**vaticinationibus**' = "prophetic utterances."　"The Germans were still further discouraged by the prophecies of their holy women, who gave oracles by peering into the eddies of rivers, and by interpreting the rolling currents and the lapping waves; they forbade battle before the new moon."　*Plutarch.*

4 '**ante novam lunam.**'　The new moon and the full moon were considered most auspicious days by the Germans (Tac. Germ. c. 11). Similarly the Spartans refused to send help to the Athenians before Marathon before the new moon.　(Herod. 6, 106.)　On the day of the new moon, see page 117.

CHAPTER LI.

1 '**postridie.**'　When Cæsar heard that the Germans despaired of victory before the new moon, he resolved to take advantage of their fear.　He brought every force to act on his side that he could, moral as well as material.

'**alarios.**'　The *alarii* were auxiliary troops of light-armed soldiers; in Cæsar's army they consisted chiefly of slingers and archers.　These troops were commonly divided into two portions, one of which served on each wing (*ala*) of the army, opening battle from a distance and retiring before fighting became close.　On this occasion Cæsar put all the *alarii* together, and drew them up in the form of legionary troops offering battle.　Meanwhile the two legions had been withdrawn from the lesser camp, probably by a secret movement, though Cæsar does not say this.　The general result would be that Ariovistus found himself assaulted by six legions, when he only expected the assault of four, and that he saw on his flank a large body apparently of legionaries, ready to take him during the fight at an advantage.

'**ad speciem**' — "to create an appearance"; *i.e.*, to induce the idea that they were legionaries.

2 '**generatim**' — "according to their tribes."　This order of battle was natural to half-civilized races, living in clanships or tribes.　It lasted long in the history of Scotland, and was employed for the last time in 1746 at Culloden.

'**Harudes.**'　See note on c. 31.7.　The *Marcomanni* are the march men, or defenders of the border; at a later time they formed a distinct tribe, but it is most probable that in Cæsar's time the name was simply appellative and not tribal, and that Cæsar made the same misconception in their case as in the case of the Suebi. The march-line, which they were charged to defend, would be the line of the Maine and Neckar, with an advanced guard in the Black Forest.

The *Triboces*, *Vangiones*, and *Nemetes* had already crossed the Rhine, and occupied the left bank from Strasburg to Spires. The *Sedusii* are doubtful.

On the *Suebi*, see Introd., pp. 7, 33.

'passis manibus' — "with outstretched hands," the attitude of 3 entreaty and exhortation."

CHAPTER LII.

'singulis legionibus.' There were six legions, of which five were 1 led by *legati;* the legati were T. Attius Labienus, L. Aurunculeius Cotta, Q. Titurius Sabinus, Q. Pedius, and S. Sulpicius Galba; the sixth, doubtless the legion commonly commanded by Cæsar in person, was under the *quæstor*, so as to leave Cæsar free, if necessary, to exercise a commander-in-chief's supervision over the whole: the heat of the struggle prevented him, it will appear, from doing this. The *quæstor* was a financial officer, his duties being to keep the military chest, give the soldiers their pay, and sell the booty; yet he might receive a military appointment; and in this case it was natural that he should, for the tie between the *quæstor* and his proconsul was very intimate, and Cæsar's work as proconsul was almost exclusively military. His *quæstor* was Marcus Crassus, son of the triumvir, and brother of Publius Crassus, mentioned a few lines below.

'ipse' = "in person." Cæsar engaged in the conflict to encourage his troops. The late mutiny had proved that their confidence in their commander was not complete.

'signo dato.' The signal to prepare for battle was a blast of the 2 trumpet (*tuba*). As the troops came within 250 yards of the enemy, the commander's ensign waved, and all the wind-instruments together (*cornua et tubae*) sounded the charge (*classicum*).

'itaque' = *et ita.*

'phalange facta' — "forming in phalanx-order." See note on 3 c. 24. 3. Each tribe formed a separate phalanx: it does not mean that the whole array formed in one phalanx.

4 ' **et desuper vulnerarent.**' Many late editors reject these words
on the ground that the action is impossible. Any single person
doing so could only have lost his life ; but why, if a number (*complures*)
leapt on the top of the flat or sloping shields together. should they
not have been able to "inflict wounds from above," and to be somewhat protected by the weight of their number ?

5 ' **multitudine.**' Had the numbers been employed in Roman
fashion to reserve their strength, and fight in turns where strength
was most required, the issue of the day might have been different :
but the rude German warrior would have thought it disgraceful to
stand idly looking on, while his kinsmen were falling in the strife.

6 ' **P. Crassus adolescens.**' P. Crassus the younger was a son of
the triumvir, and possessed great military ability. He was never a
lieutenant-general of Cæsar, yet he received several independent
and very important commands, which he executed with great skill.
After three years of service he left Gaul, and in B.C. 54 joined his
father's expedition against the Parthians. He fell on the field of
Carrhae, after refusing to save his own life and leave his men to
perish.

It is noticeable that the decisive order, by which the fight against
Ariovistus was won, did not come from Cæsar himself, but from the
younger Crassus. Cæsar apparently was in the thick of the fight
and hardly able to make the necessary dispositions at the required
moment. If this was so, he was fortunate in possessing so able an
underofficer as P. Crassus.

Chapter LIII.

1 ' **Ita** ' — "by this movement"; *i.e.*, the advance of the *tertia acies*.
' **millia quinque.**' The river five miles distant from the battlefield was probably the Ill, which at that time formed an arm of the
Rhine. On the reading, see Preface.

3 ' **profugit.**' Of the fate of Ariovistus nothing is known except
that he did not long survive. Four years afterwards (B. v. c. 29)
we are told that he was dead, and that his death rankled bitterly in
the hearts of the Germans as a cause of resentment against the
Romans.

4 ' **Duae uxores.**' Ariovistus had two wives only on account of his
high position. The German race was distinguished by respect for
the single married tie. Princes alone were allowed, or rather
requested, to have more than one wife ; relationship with them was
desired by other princes.

'utraque periit.' The butchery of women by Cæsar's soldiers has already been noticed on c. 26. 3. As his soldiers became more brutalized by the sufferings which they endured and the license which they enjoyed during the protracted war, the cruelty became even more horrible.

'trinis catenis,' *trinis* because *catenae* is a subst. almost only used 5 in the plural.

'quae quidem res.' Cæsar's natural expression of delight at 6 seeing his friend and representative again safe and sound is charming and attractive. It excites the sympathy even of Mr. Trollope, who is not wont to side with the feelings of the Proconsul.

'calamitas' = *mors*, a euphemism.

'ter,' "thrice," the sacred number. See note on c. 50. 3. 7

CHAPTER LIV.

'Suebi, qui.' See note on c. 37. 2. 1

'Ubii.' The Ubians lived on the right bank of the Rhine, from near Ems to below Cologne. They were the only German tribe who put themselves under Roman protection, and were therefore detested by their compatriots. It was probably the Ubii who supplied the cavalry which did such important service to Cæsar in his final campaign. See note on c. 48. 3.

'tempus anni.' The proper time for returning to winter- 2 quarters was the autumnal equinox, September 21st, when the *æstas*, or summer season, closed. It is not to be considered an exact date, as the actual time of the troops retiring to quarters would depend much on the state of the weather, and on their previous labours.

'in Sequanos,' *i e.* to Vesontio, to guard the frontier which they had won.

'Labienum.' By leaving Labienus in charge in his own absence, Cæsar showed that he regarded him as his chief lieutenant-general.

'conventus agendos,' "to hold his proconsular courts." 3 Cæsar was governor of Hither Gaul as well as of Further Gaul, and was bound once a year to administer justice in the chief towns of his province. He held these courts in winter, and also took advantage of the time so spent in Italy to keep himself acquainted with the web of Roman politics, and to preserve the goodwill and excite the hopes of his own partisans.

Cæsar's first campaign had decided that Gaul should be a Roman and not a German province. The Germans were driven across the Rhine, and for centuries did not venture to return. It may therefore be said with some truth, that Cæsar's victory laid the foundation of the modern history of Europe, for the connection of France with Roman traditions and language, and its contrast to Germany, has been the most essential factor in the history of Western Europe.

Cæsar had also conquered a great Celtic nation, and his army had penetrated far into the borders of hitherto independent Gaul. He had also evinced unequalled military powers, both in defensive and in offensive warfare; and similar talent in managing and playing upon the moral qualities of his opponents, and in the almost harder task of gaining a complete ascendency over his own troops.

APPENDIX.

On Oratio Recta and Obliqua.

IT is very characteristic of the Latin historic style, that continuous speeches, interspersed throughout the narrative, are not usually written in the actual words used by the speaker, but are taken out of the direct form and reported by the historian. So many reported speeches occur in the first book of Cæsar that it is necessary for the learner to grasp thoroughly the nature and rules of indirect speech, and the proper manner in which such speeches should be rendered in English.

When the words of a speech are the very words, persons, and tenses used by the speaker, it is called *Oratio Recta* or Direct Speech. and this is the form preferred by writers of English; but when the words originally used are reported, and altered in person, tense, and mood, it is called *Oratio Obliqua*, and this is the form preferred by writers of Latin.

An envoy appearing before a senate might say: "I bring you peace or war. Which do you desire? Take which you choose; thus wrangling will be at an end." This is *Oratio Recta* or Direct Speech.

Should a third person report the words, they would run: "The envoy said that he brought peace or war to them. (He asked) which they desired. Let them take which they choose; (he said) that so wrangling would be at an end." This is in *Oratio Obliqua* or Indirect Speech.

In Latin, " *Pacem vobis aut bellum affero. Utrum vultis? utrum placet, sumite; ita litium finis erit.*" Oratio Recta.

(Dixit) *Pacem se iis aut bellum afferre. Utrum vellent? utrum placeret, sumerent: ita litium finem fore.* Oratio Obliqua.

I. When the language used in conversation is reported, *the first and second persons must disappear;* all finite verbs will be in the third person. The first person will be replaced by *se, suus:* " He said that *he.*" The second person will be replaced by *is* or *ille:* " He said that he brought to *them.*"

II. *The indicative mood will disappear,* because it is the mood used in direct language ; it is the mood of a speaker or narrator and of him alone; consequently if an indicative *appears* to be used in *oratio obliqua,* it may be certain that it is not a reported verb, but in a clause inserted by the historian on his own authority.*

III. Principal Verbs, if they contain a statement, will become infinitives, because they are dependent on a *verbum declarandi.* If they are imperatives, they will change to the subjunctive mood, because they now depend on an implied verb of command. Interrogative verbs sometimes change to the subjunctive, and sometimes to the infinitive. If they are in the second person, they commonly change to the subjunctive, while the first and third persons change to the infinitive. The reason of this apparent anomaly is that all real questions become subjunctives, because they are now dependent questions: " He asked *which they desired;*" and real questions are commonly asked in the second person. But Latin writers are extremely rhetorical, and often put sentences in the form of questions, when they are in no doubt about the answer, and only use the form of a question to contain a real statement of their opinion. Such apparent questions are usually asked in the first or third person, and, when reported, are in the infinitive mood, because they really contain statements and not questions.

When the principal verb of *oratio recta* is a Deliberative Question, as *Quid faciam?* " What am I to do?" it will change only in tense and person. *Quid faceret?*

---

* On the remarkable transition from oratio obliqua to oratio recta in *cum videbatur* of c. 40, see note.

Verbs in Secondary Clauses will be altered from the indicative to the subjunctive mood; they are no longer statements for which the reporter, *i.e.* the historian, is responsible; the subjunctive mood shows that they express the thoughts of some one else, *i.e.* of the original speaker.

IV. Tenses will become Historic instead of Primary, because they now depend on an historic tense (*dixit*) expressed or implied.

V. Conditional Sentences are complex, and demand separate consideration. The common forms used in *Oratio Recta* are

(1) Where the indicative or imperative is used with the principal verb ·

Present :   *Si nescit, rogat,*
           Si nescis, roga,   reported according to the
Past :   *Si nesciebat, rogabat,*   rules already given.
           Si nesciit, rogavit,

Future :   *Si nesciet, rogabit,* reported *Dixit se, si nesciret, rogaturum esse,* but a far more common form of a future conditional is with the future-perfect; *Si nescierit, rogabit,* reported *Dixit se, si nesciisset, rogaturum esse.*

It is important to observe that the future-perfect after *si* becomes the pluperfect subjunctive, for it is very common; and that the future, by no means so common a use, becomes the imperfect subjunctive. On the other hand, questions in the future tense, when reported, are in the future subjunctive; *Quando venies ?* changes to *Quando venturus esset.* These two uses should not be confused.

(2) When both the condition and the conditional statement are in the subjunctive :

Present :

   Si sciam, non rogem. Were I to know, I should not be asking.

     This when reported becomes : *Negavit se, si sciret, rogaturum esse.*

Past :

Si scirem, non rogarem.   Had I known, I should not have
been asking.

Reported : *Negavit se, si sciret, rogaturum fuisse.*

Si audirem, respondissem.   Had I been a listener (all the
time save one was speaking), I should have answered
(in a moment).

Reported : *Dixit se, si audiret, responsurum fuisse.*

Si audiissem, respondissem.   Had I heard (a single word),
I should have answered.

Reported : *Dixit se, si audiisset, responsurum fuisse.*

Bearing these rules in mind, it will be useful to turn every
speech in this book from the indirect to the direct form. As
an example, the first speech (c. 13) is given; in *Oratio Recta,*
the actual words used by the Helvetian envoys would be :
"*Si pacem Populus Romanus cum Helvetiis faciet, in eam
partem ibimus atque ibi erimus, ubi nos constitueris atque esse
volueris; sin bello persequi perseverabis, reminiscere et veteris incommodi Populi Romani et pristinae virtutis Helvetiorum. Quod
improviso unum pagum adortus es, cum ii, qui flumen transierant,
suis auxilium ferre non possent, ne ob eam rem aut tuae magnopere virtuti tribuas aut nos despicias. Ita a patribus majoribus-
que nostris didicimus, ut magis virtute contenderemus, quam dolo
aut insidiis niteremur. Quare ne committas, ut is locus, ubi
constitimus, ex calamitate Populi Romani et internecione exercitus
nomen capiat aut memoriam prodat.*"

On the other hand it is quite as important to observe that
reported speeches can only be rendered properly in English
in the direct form. The English language possesses no
reflexive pronoun, and recoils from the ambiguities involved
in the constant "he's" and "they's" of indirect speech. As
an example of this, a translation of the 36th chapter is given,
where it will at once appear that the rude and abrupt manner
of Ariovistus is far more truly represented in English in the
direct than it could be in the indirect form.

Ariovistus replied : " The law of war is that the conqueror should rule the conquered as he pleases ; it is not the custom of Rome to rule conquered nations at another's bidding, but at her own discretion. If I do not dictate to Rome how to use her rights, I ought not to be interfered with by Rome in my rights. The Æduans appealed to arms, and met me in the field ; they were defeated, and are now my tributaries. You are doing me a great wrong, because by your appearance you are diminishing my revenues. I will not restore their hostages to the Æduans, while at the same time I will not invade them or their allies, an unprovoked wrong, so long as they abide by their agreement, and pay me their tribute year by year; if they fail to do so, it will not help them that they are called brothers by Rome. As to your threats of avenging any wrong done to the Æduans, no one ever fought with me without bringing ruin on himself. Fight me when you choose : you will find out the strength and the bravery of the Germans, true and unconquered warriors, who for fourteen years have not slept beneath a roof."

PROBABLE CHRONOLOGY OF THE
CAMPAIGN.

March 28th.	The Helvetians assemble opposite Geneva.
April 13th.	They are refused a passage.
13th-17th.	Their attempts to force Cæsar's lines.
June 7th.	(Seven weeks.) Cæsar reaches Vienna with five legions.
10th.	Battle at the Arar. Tigurini annihilated.
12th.	Passage of the river.
13th.	Divico's embassy.
13th-27th.	Fifteen days' march.
28th.	Mistake of Considius.
29th.	Battle near Bibracte.
July 8th.	Cæsar comes up with the Helvetians in the country of the Lingones.
8th-15th.	Negotiations with Gauls.
16th.	,, ,, Ariovistus (four weeks).
Aug. 12th.	Advance of the army.
18th.	Cæsar reaches Besançon.
18th-24th.	Stop at Besançon.
31st.	Reaches the Rhine-valley.
Sept. 5th.	Interview.
6th.	Second embassy of Ariovistus; arrest of Valerius and Metius.
7th-11th.	Manœuvres.
12th.	Cæsar constructs his lesser camp.
13th.	Assault on lesser camp.
14th.	Battle and defeat of Ariovistus.

Of these dates none save the first two can be known with absolute certainty. The date of the battle at Bibracte is almost certainly the 29th of June ; *omnino biduum supererat, cum exercitui frumentum metiri oporteret ;* now it is almost certain that rations were due on the first of the month ; the verse, *vos meministis quotkalendis petere dimensum cibum* (Plaut. Stich. 1, 2, 3), proves that in civil life the calends was the day for such payments, and it is probable that the same rule prevailed in military life. If rations were due on the first, the month in question must have been July, and the battle have been fought on June 29th (current calendar).

Another certain date is the new moon of September, before which Ariovistus feared to fight. Astronomers have calcu lated that it fell on the 19th (corrected calendar), the 23rd of the current calendar as corrected by von Goeler.

Cæsar says (c. 54) that he led his legions back to their quarters for the winter *maturius paulo, quam tempus anni postulabat.* The ordinary time of return was at the autumnal equinox, a date which, as has been already said in a note, must be taken with some latitude. At all events, the troops would not be due to return before Sept. 25th (the equinoctial day of the current calendar), and probably not for a few days later. Thus, if the above dates are true, the campaign was over about a fortnight before it was necessary to retire from operations in the field.

The dates of the current and uncorrected calendar have been given because the first two are certain, and the inference as to the date of the battle near Bibracte appears best under these dates. What the correct dates were is a more difficult question, on which authorities do not agree. General von Goeler makes March 28th coincide with March 24th (cor-rected calendar). Kraner, on the other hand, identifies March 28th with April 16th (corrected calendar). The latter date can hardly be correct, as the operations of the year closed before Sept. 19th (new moon of the true year) ; if they began three weeks later than the date given, it is difficult to see how they could have closed by this time. I would therefore accept the dates of von Goeler, which are followed by Napoleon.

OBSERVATIONS ON THE CAMPAIGN OF B.C. 58.

War with the Helvetians.

1. Cæsar's first military operation, the line of defence formed on the south bank of the Rhone, from Geneva to the Pas de l'Écluse, where the Jura slope comes close to the river, marked at once his ability and his decision. His object was attained, for the Helvetians were foiled both in the attempt to enter the province and to break through the lines.

2. The subsequent operations illustrate the advantages which may be obtained by military skill over a brave but uncivilized enemy. Vigilance, audacity, and promptitude are the three principles which mark Cæsar's conduct in the field.

From the start, his system of outpost service was excellent. From a distance of ten or fifteen miles he knew the position of the Helvetian camp : in his campaign with Ariovistus his explorers had been twenty-two miles in front ; the Helvetians, on the contrary, were so deficient in this service that they were surprised by the appearance of Cæsar's legions among them.

3. In the negotiations with the Æduans it may be noticed, first, that Dumnorix already divined Cæsar's purpose of subjugating Gaul, and was raising a national party in opposition. Second, that Divitiacus, a chief of the Druids, and Liscus, the representative of civil power, were alike false to their country and sided with Rome. Third, most important to the final result, is the intuition with which Cæsar grasped the position of affairs and the character of the men with whom he had to

deal. He feared Dumnorix, and, had he dared, he would have executed him at once.

4. The incident of P. Considius shows that Cæsar at the beginning of the war had the same difficulty in finding able officers that other commanders have found. It also shows that the temper of the army was more fearful than it became in subsequent years. Yet Cæsar lost a great advantage. Never, perhaps, during his later campaigns had he an enemy so completely at his mercy as on this occasion, which was thrown away by the weakness of a subordinate.

5. The final battle with the Helvetians was a great but hard-won victory. Fighting lasted for seven hours and the enemy retired in good order. No other fight was so prolonged, nor had Cæsar ever again to give his men three days' rest after a day of battle. Throughout the chief lesson is the superiority of the movable and divisible legion against the unwieldy phalanx. In the first part of the fight the Romans, standing on the defensive, could not be dislodged; the triple line could not be broken through, and yet all the forces were not employed.

In the second part, the sudden change of front to meet the Boians was the decisive point of the action. To see and meet the danger at the right moment was Cæsar's merit; but the existence of legion and cohort, bodies which could be managed and guided even in the thick of battle, alone made the movement possible.

Cæsar by removing his own horse undoubtedly did much to secure the confidence of his men. "I shall not require it till the pursuit," are the words he is said to have used. His orders that the horses of his officers and friends should be similarly removed may indicate that he already saw symptoms among his military tribunes of the spirit which burst out later in the camp at Besançon.

The advantages of the Romans lay in the ground, in their arms, for the use of the *pilum* was never more telling, in their military organization, and in their general. To these the Helvetians could only oppose a rare courage and obstinacy, and the advantage of numbers ; the system of fighting without reserves, and of trusting to one strength alone, paralyzed their real power.

6. In the disposal of the survivors it is noticeable that Cæsar's chief motive is fear of German aggression. This leads us to believe that the same feeling, dread of the Germans, had much to do with the national desire of the Helvetians to migrate from their old lands.

Operations of the Helvetians.

1. The most remarkable point in their story is the deliberation and unanimity with which they resolved in a body to leave their ancestral home. That obedience to Orgetorix, and national ambition, should have been, as Cæsar indicates, their sole motives, seems hardly possible.

2. The Helvetians were weak in allowing Cæsar to put them off for fourteen days. If they intended to pass through the province by force if necessary, they should have done so at once, instead of allowing time for the way to be blocked. Cæsar's purpose in refusing an answer could not have been friendly.

3. They lost time in negotiations and operations. While Cæsar had been to Aquileia and back, a distance of 800 miles, and had brought an army of 20,000 men into the field, they had only advanced about sixty miles from Geneva.

4. This slowness, and the deficiency of outposts, resulted in the annihilation of the Tigurine division at the passage of the Arar.

5. The embassy of the aged Divico was weak. If peace was desired, a haughty and overbearing tone should have been avoided; if war, an embassy was unnecessary. Cæsar wished for war, and Divico only played into his hands.

6. Self-confidence is again noticeable in the assault on the Roman position. Imputing Cæsar's policy to fear, *they believed what they wanted to believe*, and thus engaging at a disadvantage threw their lives away. Their indomitable courage was not able to repair the error in judgment.

The Council of Celtic Gaul.

In accepting the protectorate of Celtic Gaul against German invaders Cæsar was well aware that he was inaugurating a policy of final conquest. Without command of senate or people, he was not only going beyond his province, but accepting a dangerous war with an unknown enemy, and unlimited responsibilities towards the Celts. In his account he is at pains to show that circumstances had made this action necessary; for had he not driven |back the Germans, the Germans would have threatened Rome.

The second step appears in the order that the legions should winter among the Sequans; the feelings of discontent, undoubtedly felt universally, broke out at once in the ill-organized rising of the Belgians in the ensuing year. To Cæsar's mind, the decision of the council had made the whole of Gaul a Roman province.

He never henceforth regards any portion of the country as entitled to any liberty except such as might be conferred under the protectorate of Rome.

Campaign against Ariovistus.

1. The advantages of being first in the field are well illustrated by Cæsar's march on Besançon. The strong frontier town gave a command of the situation, for the holder of it might act on the offensive or defensive as he chose. When Cæsar gained the position, Ariovistus had to change all his plan of operation.

2. Cæsar's speech to his mutinous soldiers is a masterpiece. Calm moral and intellectual superiority, combined with the passion and subtlety of an orator, triumphed over a difficulty which would have overwhelmed a weaker leader.   Without arrogance, he claims confidence; and by an appeal to feelings of military pride and honourable rivalry, he restores the courage of his men.   His objects were gained, and gained once for all; for his soldiers never wavered again.   No chapter in the Commentaries better enables us to understand the marvellous power which Cæsar was able to wield over his men.

3. The resourcefulness shown in mounting the tenth legion should not pass unnoticed.   Cæsar was resolved that no technical or professional difficulty should interfere with the execution of an important purpose.

4. In the debates at the conference it must be allowed that Ariovistus has always the best of the argument.   The Romans had established a title in the south of Gaul, as he had in the north, where the Roman senate had acknowledged his position.   The Æduans, moreover, had undertaken not to ask Roman assistance against him.   So far as a conqueror may appeal to justice, the justice of the case lay with the German.

5. Cæsar's description of the German cavalry shows how much he admired it.   It was a force well suited for hand-to-hand combats, for it united rapidity and steadiness, and from the personal tie between the mounted and the foot-soldier must have created a remarkable *esprit de corps*.   It will afterwards appear with what great results Cæsar at a critical moment adopted a number of these warriors into his own army.

6. The lesson of the battle is similar to that of the contest with the Helvetians. The awkward phalanx was no match for the more wieldy legion.   The advance of the Roman reserve decided the day.   The rude German would have felt dis-

graced by standing idle as a reserve during hours of battle, while his brothers were shedding their blood.

7. "In all actions there is one critical and decisive moment which will give the victory to the general who knows how to seize it." *W. Napier.* This moment was observed by Publius Crassus, who, by ordering the third line to advance, decided the day.

It is rare, when a great general is in command, that the order, given at the critical moment, and obtaining victory, should proceed from anyone but himself. Cæsar had good reason to enter the press of battle, to encourage his men by his presence to stand against the Germans of whom lately they had been in fear. It is possible that while he advanced himself to share in the fighting, he left large discretionary powers with Crassus, whom he styles " more free to act."

8. The moral consequences of this victory were great over Romans, Celts and Germans. The Roman army never doubted their commander again; a single campaign had securely laid the foundation of a power which was yet to grant Cæsar supreme control over the Roman world. The Celts, freed from their oppressor, were filled with joy and gratitude, destined soon to change into apprehension, hatred and remorse. The Germans were dismayed; the Suebian hordes at once retired homewards, suffering as they went from the Ubii, over whom they had long been used to triumph. The native *Wanderlust* was checked; while Roman power survived, German invaders did not again cross the Rhine.

Operations of Ariovistus.

Ariovistus showed no mean military skill. On losing Besançon, he retired well into his own territory, where a defeat to Cæsar would have been extermination. His idea of cutting off provisions as they came up from the Æduans was sound, and might have been successful had he been able to divide his forces into two camps, as the Romans so frequently did. His large force, by operating from two centres, would have doubled its power.

Cæsar, though Dion Cassius gives a different account, says that the Germans were forced to fight. If this is so, the battle is a proof of the necessity of strong entrenchments in ancient warfare, where missile weapons were comparatively weak. " If you are a great general, come down and fight" was the taunt of the Marsian leader in the Social War to Marius ; whose reply was better, " No, if you are a great general, force me to fight against my will."

Ariovistus could not give this answer, and thus led his troops to battle under the dispiriting influence of religious fear.

FINIS.

G. NORMAN AND SON, PRINTERS, HART STREET, COVENT GARDEN, LONDON.

Williams (T. S.) Modern German and English Conversations and Elementary Phrases, the German revised and corrected by A. Kokemueller. 21st enlarged and improved Edition. 12mo. cloth   3*s* 6*d*

Williams (T. S.) and C. Cruse. German and English Commercial Correspondence. A Collection of Modern Mercantile Letters in German and English, with their Translation on opposite pages   2nd Edition. 12mo. cloth   4*s* 6*d*

Apel (H.) German Prose Stories for Beginners (including Lessing's Prose Fables), with an interlinear Translation in the natural order of Construction. 2nd edition. 12mo. cloth   2*s* 6*d*

———— **German Prose.** A Collection of the best Specimens of German Prose, chiefly from Modern Authors. A Handbook for Schools and Families. 500 pp. Crown 8vo. cloth   3*s*

𝕲erman 𝕮lassics for 𝕰nglish 𝕾chools, with 𝕹otes and 𝖁ocabulary. Crown 8vo. cloth.

Schiller's Lied von der Glocke (The Song of the Bell), and other Poems and Ballads, by M. Förster   2*s*

———— **Minor Poems.** By Arthur P. Vernon   2*s*

———— **Maria Stuart,** by Moritz Förster   2*s* 6*d*

Goethe's Hermann und Dorothea, by M. Förster   2*s* 6*d*

———— **Iphigenie auf Tauris.** With Notes by H. Attwell.   2*s*

———— **Egmont.** By H. Apel   2*s* 6*d*

Lessing's Minna von Barnhelm, by Schmidt   2*s* 6*d*

———— **Emilia Galotti.** By G. Hein   2*s*

Chamisso's Peter Schlemihl, by M. Förster   2*s*

Andersen (H. C.) Bilderbuch ohne Bilder, by Beck   2*s*

Nieritz. Die Waise, a Tale, by Otte   2*s*

Hauff's Mærchen. A Selection, by A. Hoare   3*s* 6*d*

———

Carové (J. W.) Mæhrchen ohne Ende (The Story without an End). 12mo. cloth   2*s*

Fouque's Undine, Sintram, Aslauga's Ritter, die beiden Hauptleute. 4 vols. in 1. 8vo. cloth   7*s* 6*d*

Undine. 1*s* 6*d*; cloth, 2*s*.   Aslauga. 1*s* 6*d*; cloth, 2*s*
Sintram. 2*s* 6*d*; cloth, 3*s*.   Hauptleute. 1*s* 6*d*; cloth, 2*s*

Greek, etc.

Euripides' Medea. The Greek Text, with Introduction and
Explanatory Notes for Schools, by J. H. Hogan. 8vo.
cloth   3s 6d
——— **Ion.** Greek Text, with Notes for Beginners,
Introduction and Questions for Examination, by the
Rev. Charles Badham, D.D. 2nd Edition. 8vo. 3s 6d
Æschylus. Agamemnon. Revised Greek Text, with literal
line-for-line Translation on opposite pages, by John
F. Davies, B.A. 8vo. cloth   3s
Platonis Philebus. With Introduction and Notes by Dr.
C. Badham. 2nd Edition, considerably augmented.
8vo. cloth   4s
——— **Euthydemus et Laches.** With Critical Notes, by
the Rev. Ch. Badham, D.D. 8vo. cloth   4s
——— **Convivium, cum Epistola ad Thompsonum, "De
Platonis Legibus,"** edidit C. Badham   8vo. cloth 4s

Kiepert New Atlas Antiquus. Maps of the Ancient World,
for Schools and Colleges. 6th Edition. With a complete Geographical Index. Folio, boards   7s 6d
Kampen. 15 Maps to illustrate Cæsar's De Bello Gallico.
15 coloured Maps. 4to. cloth   3s 6d

Italian.

Volpe (Cav. G.) Eton Italian Grammar, for the use of Eton
College. Including Exercises and Examples. New
Edition. Crown 8vo. cloth (Key, 1s)   4s 6d
Racconti Istorici e Novelle Morali. Edited, for the use
of Italian Students, by G. Christison. 12th Edition.
18mo. cloth   1s 6d
Rossetti. Exercises for securing Idiomatic Italian, by
means of Literal Translations from the English by
Maria F. Rossetti. 12mo. cloth   3s 6d
——— **Aneddoti Italiani.** One Hundred Italian Anec-
dotes, selected from "Il Compagno del Passeggio."
Being also a Key to Rossetti's Exercises. 12mo.
cloth   2s 6d
Venosta (F.) Raccolta di Poesie. Crown 8vo. cloth   5s

[6]

Wall Maps.

Sydow's W

Mou

1.
2.
3.
4.
5.
6.

Fyfe

Reif

De

Hebr

Attv

—————— The same Table, in 4to. with numerous Additions.
Boards   7s 6d

CPSIA information can be obtained
at www.ICGtesting.com
Printed in the USA
LVOW13s0434010817
543355LV00011B/219/P